D1332404

The Mass Media in Canada

Third Edition

Mary Vipond

James Lorimer & Company Ltd., Publishers
Toronto, 2000

Copyright © Mary Vipond

James Lorimer & Company Ltd. acknowledges the support of the Ontario Arts Council for our publishing program. We acknowledge the support of the Government of Canada through the Book Publishing Industry Development Program (BPIDP) for our publishing activities. We acknowledge the support of the Canada Council for the Arts for our publishing program.

Cover design: Kevin O'Reilly

Canadian Cataloguing in Publication Data

Vipond, Mary, 1943–
   The mass media in Canada

3rd ed.
Includes index.
ISBN 1-55028-714-1

1. Mass media – Canada – History. 2. Mass media – Social aspects – Canada. 3. Mass media – Government policy – Canada. I. Title.

P92.C3V56 2000   302.23'0971   C00-931522-5

James Lorimer & Company Ltd., Publishers
Egerton Ryerson Memorial Building
35 Britain St., 3rd Fl.
Toronto, Ontario M5A 1R7

Printed and bound in Canada.

For my parents,
Reid and Dorthy Vipond,
with gratitude and love.

Contents

Preface to the Third Edition

Many changes have occurred in the mass media industries in Canada since 1992 when this book was last revised. Most important, of course, has been the "digital revolution," especially the explosion of the Internet, and the technological, economic, cultural and regulatory fall-out from a transformation that some have likened to only two previous revolutions in communications: the inventions of writing and the printing press. I do not consider the Internet a mass medium according to my rather strict definition that embodies the dissemination of information from one central source to a vast audience with limited means of feedback. Nevertheless, it has already had — and will continue to have — a massive impact on the traditional media, changing their organizational structure and roles in ways that cannot be completely foreseen. Moreover, it is already evident that major media corporations are jockeying for control of key Internet services in ways that will likely compromise the Net's originally rather anarchic and liberating structure. The Internet is no longer only about communications; like other media it is also now about money.

One difficulty in writing this edition has been that the media industries are changing at lightning speed. It seems that every day a new merger or takeover or divestiture or stock offering is announced — virtually all of them related to positioning for digital media markets. I have endeavoured therefore to discuss general trends and principles rather than to dwell on specific details that may quickly become obsolete. The Internet has also been a blessing to me as I have prepared these revisions, in enabling quick access to many kinds of information and commentary. My thanks to Judy Appleby of Concordia Libraries for guiding me onto the Web, and once again to the editors at James Lorimer, especially Diane Young and Ward McBurney.

Introduction

In 1988, during the sometimes heated debate about whether Canada should enter into a free-trade agreement with the United States, the Regina *Leader-Post* cartoonist Brian Gable depicted a sloppy middle-aged Canadian wearing a "Miami Vice" T-shirt walking down a street adorned with McDonald's arches, Coke signs, GM and Ford dealerships, and a movie billboard advertising "Rambo XI." "What's really scary," he remarks to his wife, "is that we Canadians could lose control of our culture ...." Almost ten years later, now drawing for the *Globe and Mail*, Gable returned to the theme. The first panel of the 1997 cartoon shows the newspaper headline: "Canada to U.S. over Culture Policy: 'It's War!'" Jokey cuts of Uncle Sam trying to locate Canada in an atlas, Lucien Bouchard as a "conscientious objector" with a sweatshirt labelled "Canada is *NOT* a Culture" and the "Royal 22nd Stompin' Toms" marching to war to the tune of "Bud the Spud" follow. Finally we see a soldier-technician at a lonely telecommunications outpost reporting to his superior: "'Baywatch' successfully jammed, sir!", as the officer mutters from inside the hut: "War is Hell."[1] While the specific references are somewhat dated, the irony in these cartoons remains true and is the focus of this book. I deliberately chose the title "The Mass Media in Canada" rather than "The Canadian Mass Media" to signal the fact that much of what our media convey, especially but not only in English-speaking Canada, is not Canadian but American. There has been much talk over the years about how this situation threatens Canada's national identity by filling our minds with foreign attitudes and images and crowding out our attempts to speak to one another. But there never seems to be action that effectively rectifies it.

Why is this so? And does it matter? The answers to these questions are not completely straightforward. Interacting geographic, technological, economic and ideological factors are involved, and of course government policy decisions. The Canadian mass media developed to their present state only gradually over the course of a century that also witnessed many other changes in Canadian society. To understand the contradiction inherent in the Gable cartoons it is necessary to know more about all of these issues.

Canada is a large, diverse and divided country. It covers almost ten million square kilometres spanning six time zones. Over much of that area the terrain is so rough and the weather so difficult that little habitation can be supported. The population is therefore widely dispersed; there are fewer than three persons per square kilometre. Three out of four Canadians live in a long ribbon laid from east to west within 150 kilometres of the American border. Even along that stretch, however, there are several distinctive physical regions and significant gaps of low population density. As a consequence of these geographic factors as well as its early historical development, Canada has a highly decentralized federal system in which power is shared between the central government and those of the ten provinces and three territories. Canada is not an easy country to define, to govern or to imagine.

What is the Canadian nation? Both the concept and the traditional definition of the word "nation" developed within a European context. That definition has normally centred on the recognition of a number of characteristics that make individuals feel part of a collectivity: common ethnicity, language, history, customs and religion are most often involved. The desire of such a nation for its own sovereign state is termed "nationalism." Canada is clearly not a nation in quite this sense. While we do have our own independent state it was more "thrust upon us" than fought for. It also encompasses many ethnic groups, two official languages, a largely colonial history, diverse customs and religions, and a relatively high proportion of recent immigrants. Additionally, the language of the majority of Canadians is the same as that of our nearest neighbouring country. While in some respects the French-speaking part of Canada has more of the characteristics of a "nation" than either the English-speaking or the whole, for Quebec, too, many qualifications are necessary.

How then can we define Canadian culture? Because culture is deeply (although not exclusively) rooted in the exchanges facilitated by language, Canada's language duality has led most to the conclusion that we have not one but two cultures. But the difficulty goes deeper. "Bilingualism" and "biculturalism," the watchwords of the 1960s, were supplemented by "multiculturalism" and "regionalism" in the 1970s and 1980s, and "downsizing" and "globalization" in the 1990s. The daunting task of conceptualizing a Canadian nationality and/or culture has baffled so many over the years that there is more than a little truth to the joke that the common thread in our national culture is quite simply our never-ending "search for identity."

The root of the problem lies in the fact that Canada was created in 1867 as a political and economic entity for pragmatic and imperial rather than nationalist reasons. Only after the formation of the Canadian state out of several different colonies was the attempt to create a Canadian nation begun. One of the principal means by which national unity was promoted was by the construction of networks of communication, beginning with the Canadian Pacific Railway (CPR).

"Communication" has remained central to both the material and the mythological definition of Canada ever since. As Robert Fulford put it, "communications influence all societies, but Canada in particular takes its shape and meaning from communications systems."[2] That two of our world-recognized scholars, Harold Innis and Marshall McLuhan, both developed theories of communication and technology is not viewed as a coincidence. Neither is it surprising that a number of Canadian students of nationalism have been attracted to the "functional" theory of Karl Deutsch, who posited that nationalism depends not so much on shared characteristics as on the fact that members of the same nation "communicate more effectively, and over a wider range of subjects, with members of one large group than with outsiders"[3] (although that definition, too, suggests that French and English are two nations within a single state). Continually, and at times desperately, seeking common bonds, Canadian politicians, scholars, poets and even businessmen have all contributed to this idea (or myth[4]) that Canada is a country built by and still dependent upon, communications and communications technology. The voyageurs, the CPR, the Canadian Broadcasting Corporation (CBC), the Trans-Canada Highway and Anik satellites are all essential parts of that mythology. The major reason the state of our mass media is a matter of such concern and contention is the centrality of the idea of communications in the Canadian social imagination.

Communication lines, however, do not run only east-west. Canada's geographical position sharing a 9,000-kilometre border with the leading English-speaking world power, ten times as populous, has also been a crucial determinant in our national development. The first large influx of English-speaking Canadians were Loyalists from the thirteen American colonies, and bonds of origin, family, tourism, trade and defence have tied Canada and the United States together ever since. The first Canadian telegraph and railroad lines were constructed for cross-border rather than internal purposes, for example, and goods, people and ideas have moved in both directions across the border for two centuries.

From common circumstances and constant interchange have come many social and intellectual similarities between Canadians and Americans. One of the most important things we share is a common assumption that may be labelled "liberal developmentalism."[5] Throughout their histories both countries have devoted themselves to extracting the resources of a well-endowed continent for the enrichment of all, especially the private entrepreneurs who promoted the ventures. Much has been written by Canadian scholars about how we have historically been more conservative, more cautious, more collectively oriented, more willing to let government take charge, than the Americans. While there is some truth to this perception, and while we do have a more mixed economy and a more welfare-oriented state, it must not blind us to the fact that we also share the major liberal and free-enterprise assumptions and goals of Americans.

In a number of interesting studies historian Allan Smith has demonstrated how by the end of the nineteenth century the traditional collective and conservative world-view of English Canada had been almost completely replaced by the liberal, individualist, free-enterprise ideology of the United States.[6] Both English and French Canadians today largely accept the core ideas in this belief system, most particularly the notion that the needs of all are most efficiently provided for when goods and services are free to compete in the open marketplace, despite overwhelming evidence that that marketplace is now dominated by multinational monopolies. A most important corollary to the idea of economic laissez-faire is the belief in a free press, not government-controlled but privately financed, as the medium for the interchange of competing ideas and therefore the bastion of democratic government. A second key corollary is the assumption (if not the reality) that all citizens are equal, and are to be treated equally, particularly in their relations with the government.

The current state of our mass media, largely Canadian-owned but filled with American content, can best be understood as the product of the tensions within and between these two Canadian idea systems, the myth of communications and the ideology of liberal individualism. For the most part, the mass media have developed in Canada in the private sector, as profit-seeking enterprises, because of the prevailing liberal belief in freedom of the press. The natural economic consequence of private media-ownership has been a tendency to reduce expenses by importing American content. Governments have intervened only very cautiously for the same liberal reasons. Equally, however, the desire to foster communication links in a large and disparate country has led the federal government from time to time to encourage, support or actually construct communication facilities deemed essential to national purposes that private enterprise cannot profitably provide. Ironically, these government-fostered distribution systems have frequently been used to carry privately induced, and often American, messages.

Thus Canada has found itself in the anomalous position of having one of the most highly developed mass-media systems in the world, which serves to a considerable extent as a conduit for the distribution of non-Canadian cultural goods. Canadians believe simultaneously in liberal individualism and technological salvation. These ideas are basic to what it means to be Canadian; they also make it extremely difficult, however, given our geographical and historical situation, to remain Canadian.

This book will analyze how these fundamental contradictions have moulded our mass media into their present form. The first three chapters outline the historical evolution of the five major mass media — daily newspapers, general-interest magazines, movies, radio and television. The next three deal consecutively and in detail with economic, cultural and technological issues. The final chapter will examine the ways in which Canadian governments have intervened to attempt to make the mass media serve various national goals.

The Rise of the Mass Media

The first mass medium in Canada was the urban daily newspaper. Beginning in the last third of the nineteenth century and culminating around the time of the First World War, Canadian city newspapers evolved from small, politically oriented, low-circulation journals to the bulky, diverse and widely read papers that are commonplace today. In the same period the mass magazine arrived in Canada. Initially imported from the United States, the mass magazine had become indigenous to Canada by the mid 1920s as well. The rise of these mass media was the result of an interaction among a number of phenomena that transformed the Canadian economy, social structure and cultural milieu in the years between 1850 and 1920. The principal factors that led to the "modernization" of Canada in this period, and the consequent (and contributing) growth of the mass newspaper and magazine were external influence, industrialization, urbanization, technological change, and the growth of literacy and leisure.

The Early Canadian Press

The early centuries of Canadian development, first under the French and then the British, were devoted to beginning the exploitation of the country's vast resources for export abroad. In such a pioneering society, there was little surplus money or time for sophisticated cultural or intellectual endeavour, and so what there was was largely imported. Quebec's élite depended upon France for books, periodicals, cultural trends and ideas, English Canada's on Britain. Gradually over the course of the nineteenth century, as the United States flourished both economically and culturally, English Canadians increasingly looked southward for their cultural products, especially more popular material like romantic novels and poems. Given the common border between the two countries, the fact that the majority shared the English language, and especially because of the social similarities that were a product of their common pioneering lifestyle, this was not surprising.

The continuous and widespread import of French, British and American cultural goods in the nineteenth century did not mean, of course, that Canada produced none of her own. No printing presses had been allowed in New France because of French authorities' fears that they could not control them, but in the British colony of Nova Scotia Canada's first newspaper, the Halifax *Gazette*, began publication in 1752. Almost immediately after the British Conquest American printers brought presses into Quebec; the bilingual Quebec *Gazette* was founded in 1764 by two Philadelphia printers and the Montreal *Gazette du Commerce et Littéraire* in 1778. Newspapers were the first indigenous print medium because they provided current local commercial and official information, a role that could not be fulfilled by imports.

While these very early newspapers and others like them met a real need, their heavy dependence on government support and patronage precluded the publication of material critical of authority. Only after about 1815, as various factions in all the colonies began debating the form of British rule, did political controversy and criticism begin to appear in the newspapers. By Confederation, it seemed that they contained little else. Virtually every paper (and by 1857 there were 291 of them in British North America, most issued weekly or bi-weekly) was allied with either the Conservative or Reform (Liberal) cause, aiding and abetting the favoured party's stance, and then benefitting from the patronage of government printing or advertising contracts when it won power. Not only editorials but news stories openly championed party causes. One example will suffice. In 1882 young newsman P.D. Ross was sent by his editor at the Toronto *Mail* (a Conservative paper) to cover an election meeting. His story, published inadvertently, gave equal prominence to the claims and promises made by both the Liberal and the Conservative candidates. The head editorial writer denounced young Ross furiously: Didn't he know that the "Liberals were a bad bunch and not worth giving any publicity to?"[1] The tradition of a partisan press was to remain strong in Canada until well into the twentieth century. It remained, however, a press that appealed mainly to an élite readership; lacking a powerful working class movement, no strong labour press ever developed in Canada.

The local and transient nature of the kind of material that appears in newspapers necessitated their publication in the Canadian colonies from the earliest days. This was not the case with magazines (which may be distinguished from newspapers in that they have separate paper covers and are usually issued less frequently). While the earliest Canadian magazine, the *Nova Scotia Magazine and Comprehensive Review of Literature, Politics and the News*, was published for the edification of about two hundred subscribers in the late eighteenth century, until almost the end of the nineteenth century Canadian magazines were distinguished mainly by the brevity of their existence and the derivative nature of their contents. Being more expensive, and almost exclusively literary, magazines were read primarily by the small upper middle-class élite of the colonies. As it did not much matter if they were six weeks or two months out of date, British periodicals remained popular far into the nineteenth century. By the 1880s many middle-class English Canadians read the "better" American periodicals like *Harper's* and *Scribner's* as well, and the less prosperous read the cheap "sentimental stories" type of American magazine. The few struggling Canadian magazines often simply imported their articles. Even when they did publish local writers, the material was for the most part imitative of the styles and subject-matter of the cultural metropoli of London, Paris, New York and Boston. Again, the situation is hardly surprising. Before this century, Canada lacked the large urban centres, cosmopolitan population, surplus wealth and cultured middle class necessary to produce much by way of its own original magazine literature.

The Late-Nineteenth-Century Transformation

The transformation of Canada's economy and society — and of its media — began, most historians would say, in the 1850s. As economic and communications historian Harold Innis argued many years ago, Canada has always been dependent for its existence on lines of transportation stretching from the east coast inland toward the heartland of rich natural resources. Initially, of course, the St. Lawrence River, the Great Lakes, and the other river systems stretching west and north provided the vital arteries for the growth of the fur, lumber and wheat staples upon which Canada's economy was founded. But rivers (as well as the supplementary canal system developed after the 1820s) have the great disadvantage in our climate of being frozen many months of the year. While a few primitive roads were hacked through the forest, neither they nor the vehicles that could travel them were suitable for carrying the bulky export products to the sea. The breakthrough occurred with the arrival of the railway. In the 1850s, using technology developed in Britain and engineers imported from the United States, the Canadian colonies began to supplement the waterways with railways. By the end of the decade there were 1,000 miles of railway line laid in what is now Canada; by Confederation there were 2,500; by 1885 the railroad ran from Halifax to Vancouver.

Not only did the railways enable better movement of export staples, they also speeded up the circulation of goods, people and ideas within Canada. They were the key to the economic, political and cultural integration upon which the creation of a Canadian nation depended. Newspapers and magazines, for their part, played a central role in that integrative process. With improved transportation, they could be much more widely distributed than before, and much more cheaply. Material to fill the pages could also be acquired more quickly.

Almost simultaneously with the beginning of the railway age, the telegraph was developed. By 1850 all the major eastern cities were linked by telegraph wires to each other and to major American centres. Newspapers soon became some of the biggest customers of the telegraph companies, and the political and business information in their pages became both fuller and timelier. The completion of the undersea cable across the North Atlantic in 1866 made possible rapid access to European commercial and political news as well. Thus the publication of regular daily editions of newspapers became feasible for the first time. All in all, the mid-century communications revolution, the result of the spread of the railway and the telegraph across Canada's under-populated wilderness, opened up undreamed-of opportunities for the Canadian commercial economy, the Canadian state and the Canadian press.

The building of the railways had other profound effects as well. For the most part the rolling stock (engines and cars), rails and other equipment and machinery necessary for the extensive railway building spree were manufactured in Canada. As a result, steel mills, metal works and numerous other machine-oriented establishments were erected in Canadian centres that had previously seen little industrial enterprise beyond flour, sugar and lumber mills (processing primary products) and the production of textiles, shoes and other basic consumer goods by craftsmen. Additionally, the arrival of the railroad enabled the best or luckiest manufacturers to expand production to serve markets beyond their local communities, while the acquisition of improved metalworking techniques also enabled them to build machinery to mechanize the production processes for food, textiles, shoes and so on. Domestic production was encouraged by federal government legislation, particularly by the National Policy tariffs instituted after 1879. Markets for the products of the burgeoning factories were developed by continuing expansion of the rail network and through increasingly sophisticated distribution networks and advertising techniques.

Although the years 1873–1896 have traditionally been categorized as a period of economic depression in Canada, during this time the infrastructure of industrialization gradually was built up in Canada's major cities: Montreal, Toronto, Hamilton, Saint John and Halifax. By the end of the century production had become more concentrated in a few centres, in Ontario and Quebec, and consolidated in ever-larger plants and companies. The boom of the first decade of the twentieth century and the large-scale manufacture of munitions and other war-related goods during the First World War capped the evolution of the Canadian economy to full industrial maturity.

As industrial production grew, so did the demand for workers. Immigrants arriving from across the Atlantic and migrating rural Canadians began to swell the population of the cities and to find employment in their factories. Montreal grew from 144,000 to 360,000 between 1871 and 1901; Toronto expanded from 115,000 to 238,000 in the same period. By 1921 their populations were 618,500 and 522,000 respectively, and Winnipeg, Vancouver, Hamilton and Ottawa all had over 100,000 residents. Almost 54 per cent of Canadians lived in urban areas by 1931.

In the rapidly growing cities greater specialization of occupations was possible. Among other things, this meant that cultural interests could be better served because of the concentration of audiences and producers. More obviously, the character of the urban population changed and diversified. Many of the new arrivals were semi-skilled and unskilled workers, a new (and for many members of the middle class rather frightening) addition to the civic scene. Working long hours at often dirty and dangerous tasks in unsafe conditions prompted a militancy that expressed itself in late-nineteenth and early-twentieth century Canadian cities by the formation of unions and the development of an incipient working-class consciousness. By 1920 Canada was a modern industrial nation: much bigger, wealthier and more sophisticated than seventy years earlier, but also (or so it seemed to many) more divided, less tranquil and less moral. Most important, perhaps, the values and attitudes by which many

Canadians lived and measured their lives were no longer those of a traditional society dominated by agriculture and trade but were urban, and growth- and progress-oriented.

A caution must be inserted here. The process that has just been described did not of course happen smoothly or at an even pace in different parts of the country. Neither was it a complete transformation; many elements of the traditional, both in the economy and the society, persisted for a long time. Thus, the largest sector of the labour force remained employed in agriculture and primary extraction (for example lumbering and mining) well into the 1930s. Nevertheless, a significant change in priorities, in dominant modes of life and values, did occur between 1850 and 1920. From being mainly agricultural and traditional, Canada became primarily urban and modern over the course of those seventy years.

A modern industrial state needs not only a large workforce, it needs a trained one. Parallel with, and in some cases even preceding, the growth of industrial Canada came an increasing demand for education for all. Able workers were not the only goal; the middle-class reformers who initiated the campaign for the broadening of educational opportunities in the mid-nineteenth century also viewed schooling as a solution to the problems of poverty, crime and lack of social cohesion which so worried them. They sought not simply to improve literacy but to develop the qualities necessary for a productive Canadian workforce — diligence, obedience, promptness, honesty and so on — and to divert or repress any tendencies toward class consciousness or radical struggle on the part of the workers. In other words, as the historians put it, they viewed the schools as instruments of social control. It may also be argued that the reformers saw the schools as tools of "state formation," that is, as agencies that taught people how to live with one another in a civil community by inculcating such virtues as toleration, cooperation and respect for authority.[2]

The first signs of the new stress on education for all came after the 1840s in Canada West (Ontario) with the passage of a series of school acts that culminated in the act of 1871 requiring each municipality to provide a free common school, and compelling all children aged 7 to 12 to attend school at least four months of the year. Similar laws were passed in most provinces in the late nineteenth century.

It was one thing to pass such legislation, it was another to really make it work. The latter demanded not just laws and money but, even more important, sufficient social change that farmers and workers alike would be willing to sacrifice their children's labour for the sake of schooling. One measure of the ultimate success of the project is the gradually rising rates of literacy. While the statistics kept in Canada are less than perfect, it seems that overall the literacy rate rose from about 70 per cent in 1850 to about 90 per cent in 1900 and 95 per cent in 1921. Generally, city dwellers were more literate; as early as 1871 in Toronto 95.6 per cent of men could read and write, while the figure for all of Ontario was 88.7 per cent. Literacy lagged in the province of Quebec compared with the English provinces, due to a late start caused by the indifference of the Catholic Church and to an economic structure that still encouraged child labour. Only 53.3 per cent of males in that province were literate in 1871. Even in Quebec, however, the general literacy rate had reached 78 per cent by 1901 (using that census's rather unfortunate categorization which included all over the age of five). Yet, although most Canadians by 1900 possessed the ability to read and write, the skill of many was still at a fairly rudimentary level. As late as the 1930s only about two-thirds of Canadian children finished elementary school, and only one out of five graduated from high school.

Finally, the industrial system produced, for the workers, a certain amount of leisure. The word leisure has been defined by scholars in two main ways. Classically, it has been synonymous with cultivation, self-enrichment and learning — thus the etymology of the Greek word for leisure, "schole," which is the origin of our word school, and the early-19th-century concept of the "leisure classes." More commonly today the word is used simply to mean "free" or discretionary time, or more specifically, time not expended in making a living. The concept of leisure as something clearly distinct from work is a product of the Industrial Revolution. In the Middle Ages, the lower orders usually worked only about two days in three, the other days being taken up with festivals, religious holidays and so on. But the way of life was so integrated and communal that it possessed patterns and rhythms quite unlike our notion of work days versus holidays. For one thing, everyone was expected to participate in the holiday celebrations; in that sense they did not represent "free time." Similarly, in early pioneering Canada, the farmer's work and non-work hours were not clearly distinguished, nor were the urban artisan's, in part because the workplace was often also the home.

With industrialization, however, work became more regularized and more disciplined: it began and ended at certain hours; it occurred on separate premises; and workers were no longer allowed to relax on the job. A British factory inspector wrote in 1859:

> The distinction [is] at last made clear between the worker's own time and his master's. The worker knows now when that which he sells is ended, and when his own begins; and, by possessing a sure foreknowledge of this, is enabled to prearrange his own minutes for his own purposes.[3]

As competition increased at the end of the nineteenth century, managers began to demand even greater productivity and efficiency from their workers. The trade-off, however, was that the workers were completely free from their tasks and their bosses once they left their place of employment. They now had leisure time — free time — with which they could do anything they wanted. In the hundred years since then, the work week has steadily shrunk, from an average of seventy hours to forty. Leisure time has increased proportionally (although in the era of 1990s downsizing it began to shrink again for some segments of the population). The creation of leisure resulted in the parallel creation of institutions devoted to filling up people's leisure hours, among them, the mass media.

Thus it was in this context of industrialization, urbanization, improved means of transportation and communication, the growth of the working class and increased literacy and leisure — in sum, of "modernization" — that the mass media were born. It is debatable, however, which was cause and which effect. Many scholars argue that the existence of the mass media *led to* the rise of literacy, rather than the reverse. Equally, many see the media as at least as much the spreaders of modernization — of the secular, urban notion of living in the here and now, on a daily or hourly schedule — as the product of that transformation.

Either way, the mass media played a mediating role as one of the principal institutions by which individuals were taught to cope with the transition from traditional to modern, and to find a comfortable compromise between them. They helped people make sense of their lives in a rapidly changing world. From another point of view they also acted, like the school, as agents of social control and state formation, by which the newly urban masses were taught the "classless" values necessary to their orderly integration into a new national society.

The Daily Newspaper

As we have seen, newspapers existed in the English colonies in Canada from their earliest days. By Confederation they were an important part of the life of the country, especially the political and business life. Between 1870 and 1920, however, fundamental changes occurred in the readership, ownership, financing, production, style and contents of Canadian newspapers which turned them into our first truly mass medium. More precisely, this transformation occurred in the daily newspapers of the larger cities; it was less evident in the journals in smaller towns and rural areas that also proliferated during this period.

The harbinger of newspaper modernization was the "New Journalism" or "people's press" of Great Britain and the United States in the 1830s and 1840s.[4] In that period certain entrepreneurial newspaper owners, faced with vicious competition, had begun to shake free of traditional partisan ties and to produce newspapers geared more to the needs, interests and reading-level of the new urban masses. Their reasoning was straightforward. To maintain profitability more readers were needed; the rapidly growing population of city dwellers was the obvious market. It no longer made sense to limit the potential readership to those in agreement with the platform of one political party, or even to those interested in politics. The significance was deeper, however. These publishers were first and foremost businessmen, not aspiring players of the political game. They were, in fact, industrialists. They identified a product with potential demand, developed manufacturing techniques to produce it in large quantities, advertised it, competed head-on with others for customers, and, eventually, consolidated and even monopolized segments of the marketplace.

The same phenomenon occurred in Canada, although somewhat later and on a more subdued scale. George Brown's Toronto *Globe*, founded in 1844, was in a certain sense Canada's first "modern" newspaper. Although thoroughly allied with the Reform cause, Brown ambitiously sought to expand the *Globe*'s readership beyond party loyalists. He increased the frequency of the paper (by 1853 it was a daily), expanded its size, published a weekly edition for subscribers who lived outside Toronto, introduced a cheaper evening edition and installed the latest press equipment. His reward was an increase in circulation from 18,000 to 45,000 between 1856 and 1872 (for the daily and weekly editions combined). Nevertheless, Brown's

Globe remained traditional in its content (politics) and style (vituperative). It remained for another generation to take the next step toward the truly mass newspaper.

The first really popular daily in Canada was the Montreal *Star*, founded in 1869. Others soon emerged: the Toronto *Telegram* in 1876, Toronto *World* (1880), Toronto *News* (1881), Montreal's *La Presse* in 1884, the Ottawa *Journal* (1885), Hamilton *Herald* (1889), and by no means least, the Toronto *Star* in 1892. These papers were the personal kingdoms of Canada's first newspaper tycoons: Hugh Graham (Lord Atholstan), John Ross Robertson, Trefflé Berthiaume, E.E. Sheppard, Billy Maclean, P.D. Ross, Joseph Atkinson. Colourful and enterprising, these entrepreneurs produced newspapers which reflected their idiosyncratic views and styles. Hugh Graham used the Montreal *Star*, for example, as his platform for fighting flamboyant crusades against the establishment. In 1888 he created what he called "The Star's Pick and Shovel Brigade" to clean off Montreal's dirty streets; during the 1885 smallpox epidemic he personally ordered out the militia to free the Exhibition Building for use as a hospital. Similarly, when E.E. Sheppard was in control of the Toronto *News* he specialized in titillating gossip columns, hoaxes and a campaign for the "total Americanization" of Canada's political system.[5] As newspaper publishers freed themselves from political alliances, they were increasingly able to indulge their personal views.

A number of characteristics distinguished these popular dailies, to a greater or lesser degree, from the older party journals (which continued to exist, but which catered to a more traditional middle-class readership). To a large extent, the Canadian mass dailies deliberately copied the successful formula previously developed by such American publishers as James Gordon Bennett and William Randolph Hearst.

First, these newspapers and their proprietors were "independent"; they favoured no particular political party. They claimed to act as watchdogs against corruption or conspiracy in either party, and supported generally reformist causes appealing to the working man, including manhood suffrage, shorter working hours, public ownership of utilities and so on.

Secondly, most of these papers were evening editions, more convenient for those who worked under close supervision from the early morning on. They were to be read in the leisure hours after work. Most of them sold for one cent, while the more respectable morning papers cost two or three. Often they were sold by newsboys and at newsstands, whereas previously most newspapers had been available only by subscription. In 1894 the Montreal *Herald* even introduced streetcorner coinboxes. While primarily oriented to the urban market, many of the dailies also targeted subscribers in nearby rural hinterlands by offering cheap yearly subscriptions. Service to these customers was facilitated by good train service and low second-class mail rates, which the publishers were able to persuade the federal government to subsidize for the sake of an "enlightened" citizenry.

Thirdly, both in style and in content, these popular dailies were attractive, simple and direct. Gradually the solid eight columns of print common in the early newspapers began to be broken up with two- or three-column headlines, more white space and illustrations. Advertising was moved off the front page, replaced by the major news stories of the day. By the end of the First World War banner headlines in large type and photographs were commonplace, so that the papers essentially *looked* like the ones we see today. The papers expanded from four pages to eight, twelve, sixteen, even more on weekends. The writing style was chattier, breezier, not as pompous or literary as in the more traditional journals. The principal emphasis was on facts and information, much of it trivial. Always, the local angle was the most important, and by the 1920s whole armies of reporters were hired by papers like the Toronto *Star* to provide saturated coverage of the local scene. The strong secondary emphasis was on entertainment, both in sensational and human-interest news stories and in an increasing number of "features" designed to appeal to different groups of readers. At *La Presse*, to cite one example, the proportion of total news space devoted to political opinions fell from about 14 per cent to less than 4 per cent between 1885 and 1914, while space devoted to sports and leisure rose from 5 per cent to over 15 per cent.[6] Many of the new features, which included serialized novels, science columns, sports news, women's pages and comics, were purchased as "boiler-plate," pre-set type forms usually acquired from American syndicates. Above all, these newspapers featured diversity in their contents, so as to appeal to as much of the heterogeneous population of the modern Canadian city as possible.

The success of these popular journals was undeniable. Between 1880 and 1890 the Montreal *Star*'s circulation grew from 15,000 to over 30,000; by 1900 it was over 57,000 and by 1920 106,000. *La Presse* did even better. Founded in the mid-1880s, it had a circulation of over 20,000 by 1891 and was the top-selling daily in Canada by 1900, with a circulation of over 67,000. By 1920 it sold over 125,000 copies a day. Similarly, the Toronto *Telegram* went from 5,000 in 1878 to almost 25,000 by 1889 and 94,000 by 1920.

As the circulations of these popular newspapers rose, many of them became large enterprises. Railways and other corporate interests provided (often secretly) the capital necessary for continued expansion. The editorial independence and reformism of the newspapers began to slip away as they became linked to promoters trying to obtain contracts, subsidies and franchises from local, provincial and federal governments. Publishers became important businessmen, interested in wielding, or trying to wield, political influence in a world in which business and politics were closely intertwined. The press was now another big business, integrated into both Canada's corporate structures and its political deal-making. Newspapers were no longer partisan in the sense that they were merely the mouthpieces of the parties; rather, their financial resources gave the publishers new clout to act as independent forces within the political parties, in their own interest and that of their business allies.[7] In the process, the papers lost much of their individuality and flamboyance, but they did retain the stylistic changes of the previous twenty years, including more "professional" non-partisan reporting in the news columns.

At the same time, the more middle-class newspapers, beset by ferocious competition from their popular rivals, gradually adopted many of their techniques of style and content, and began aggressively seeking readers outside party confines as well. This trend accelerated after the turn of the century. In 1909, there were still forty-five dailies in Ontario that loudly proclaimed their party affiliation, and only nine that stated that they were independent (although these nine had proportionately large circulations); by 1930–1, those figures were almost reversed: only eleven remained partisan and twenty-five labelled themselves independent.[8] The more traditional dailies also grew considerably, if not as rapidly as the splashy popular journals. Thus by 1900 the *Globe* reached a circulation of 47,000, and its rival the *Mail and Empire* 41,000. By 1920 the figures were 88,000 and 80,000 respectively. Many new papers were established in this period as well, particularly as the western provinces were settled, among them the Victoria *Colonist* (1858), Manitoba *Free Press* (1872), Calgary *Herald* (1883), Regina *Leader* (1883), and two Vancouver papers, the *Sun* (1886) and the *Province* (1894).

Clearly, overall newspaper readership grew phenomenally in the late nineteenth and early twentieth century. This was the result of the coincidence of two factors: more Canadians became newspaper readers, and those who were readers bought more papers each day. In 1872 (taking into account the circulation of both daily and weekly editions), less than one-half of Canadian families purchased a daily newspaper; by 1900 more papers were sold each day than there were families in the nation. By 1911 in some larger cities the average family took two and a half papers per day.[9] By the measure of readership, then, the daily newspaper was a mass medium by the turn of the century. And by other measures as well: it provided a hetero-geneous urban population with news, information, and entertainment stirred deliberately into a mix that would interest and inform the greatest possible number of readers simultaneously.

Advertising

Behind these advances in sales and readership lay fundamental changes in the economics of the newspaper business. The popular newspapers were from the beginning dependent on two principal sources of income: advertising and circulation sales. While the par-tisan press also had access to government patronage, by the late nineteenth century printing contracts and the like constituted only a small part of their income; they, too, had to rely primarily on sales and advertising.

Advertising is as old as newspapers in Canada. The very first advertisements appeared in the Halifax *Gazette* on March 23, 1752: one for butter, one for a lawyer's services, and the third for instruc-tion in "Spelling, Reading, Writing in all it's [sic] different Hands...."[10] By the 1850s advertising filled anywhere from one-third to two-thirds of the typical colonial newspaper, usually concentrated on the front and back pages. Much of it consisted of commercial notices for local businesses, but there were also "consumer" ads for products like patent medicines, coal and clothing. The advertise-ments were dull and staid; extravagant claims were frowned upon (except in the patent medicine ads), and only the very occasional line drawing broke up the rows of type.

A typical ad in the *Montreal Herald and Daily Commercial Ga-zette* on February 4, 1863, for example, used only different type sizes to attract attention. "FURS! FURS! FURS!" it began, "A great variety of Choice Furs is now ready for inspection at A. BRAHADI'S First Prize Fur Establishment. Any one desirous of securing a FIRST-RATE ARTICLE will do well to call and examine the extensive Stock before purchas-ing elsewhere." The ad concluded (revealing that it had been running unaltered ever since the previous October): "Also On Hand A Large

Assortment of HATS AND CAPS For the Fall Wear." Similarly, a patent medicine ad in the *Newbrunswick Reporter* on October 16, 1846 ran three-quarters of a column in small type. Beginning with a series of testimonials from clergymen and minor British nobility, the ad for Holloway's Pills proclaimed that "THE MIGHTY POWERS OF THESE EX-TRAORDINARY PILLS WILL DO WONDERS IN ANY OF THE FOLLOWING COM-PLAINTS," and then listed (in alphabetical order) a total of thirty-six ailments ranging from "ague," asthma and "bilious complaints" to "fits," piles, tumours, ulcers and "worms of all kinds." The medicine was also apparently effective for "venereal affections" and "female irregularities," the latter being recognizable to readers as a hint that it induced abortions.

While these advertisements may seem quaint to the modern eye, they were essential both to the publishers and to other businessmen of early Canada. Ad revenue constituted less than half the total income of newspapers in this period, but few could have survived without it. Reciprocally, the newspaper was by far the most wide-spread and therefore most useful advertising medium in the colonial town or city.

As the century progressed, advertising became an even more im-portant part of the modernizing newspaper. By 1900 about two-thirds of the typical newspaper consisted of ads. The advertisements changed in character and format with the rise of the mass newspaper: more and more white space, more attractive illustrations, more gim-micks. After about 1870, department stores began to place full-page advertisements, often a couple of times a week, and their business became highly prized by the publishers. Separate classified ad sec-tions also were created after about 1870; the Toronto *Telegram* was famous for its one-cent-a-word classifieds, which added to its local market appeal. Most important, from the 1890s brand-name adver-tising of frequently used items like liquor, tobacco and processed foods became common, encouraging both the middle classes and the masses to purchase the many products being churned out by the expanding factories of North America. National manufacturers needed the mass media as vehicles to convince consumers to buy products that were often differentiated by little more than their pub-licity claims.

Advertising consequently became increasingly central to the fi-nancing of newspaper publication. Historian Paul Rutherford has calculated, for example, that 67.9 per cent of the income of the Ottawa *Citizen* in 1900 came from ads, 65.5 per cent of that of the

Hamilton *Spectator* in 1902, and 76.1 per cent of that of the Toronto *News* in 1906.[11] By the First World War a newspaper needed to fill at least 60 to 65 per cent of its space with advertising to be profitable. This dependency was basic to the structure of the modernizing newspaper business. Subscribers were desired, not for the pennies they paid to buy the daily paper, but because the larger the circulation, the more advertising dollars attracted. In effect, by the early twentieth century, a double transaction was taking place: publishers were simultaneously selling newspapers to readers and selling audiences to advertisers. The former occurred for the sake of the latter.[12]

The pursuit of advertising revenue thus shaped the mass newspaper. It meant, for example, that virtually any measure would be taken to expand circulation and was therefore a principal motive for the stylistic changes that popularized and diversified the contents of Canadian newspapers in the late nineteenth century. It also lay behind frequent subscription price cuts — which in turn of course only increased the dependence on advertisers. Give-aways were also commonly used to expand circulation; all sorts of prizes, ranging from books and alarm clocks to trips to Europe, were offered to those who could sign up new subscribers.

Thus by the end of the nineteenth century the mass newspaper and the advertiser were interdependent: the publisher earned the bulk of his revenue from ads, the advertisers of the new mass-consumer products gained access to potential purchasers. Newspaper publishers were now as tied to advertisers as their predecessors had been to government patronage.

Technological Change

One final factor crucial to the development of the mass newspaper must be mentioned: technology. Technological change both inspired and enabled the transformation of the partisan colonial journal into a mass medium.

Canada's earliest newspapers were printed on small wooden hand-operated flat-bed presses using paper manufactured from linen and cotton rags. In the 1840s iron presses driven by steam power were introduced; a decade later revolving cylinder (rotary) presses that could print up to 6,000 impressions per hour became available. The *Globe* led in introducing the new machinery into Canada; in 1867, for example, it purchased a Hoe Lightning Press capable of printing 10,000 impressions an hour. In 1880 it installed an even more advanced web press. Fed by a continuous roll of newsprint, printing both sides of the page simultaneously, and attached to a device that folded the papers automatically, this machine could print and fold 28,000 copies of an eight-page paper in one hour.

Revolutions in type-setting and paper-making occurred in the late nineteenth century as well. While previously type had to be painstakingly set by hand, letter by letter, after the introduction of the linotype in the early 1890s the compositor could sit at a keyboard setting up a whole automatically justified line at a time. A task that had previously taken five hours now took one. New forms for setting up the whole page made breaking up columns with dramatic headlines and inserting engravings and photographs easier as well. Colour printing also became possible by the turn of the century. Meanwhile, in the early 1860s, with rag paper becoming increasingly expensive, new processes were invented for the manufacture of paper out of woodpulp. By 1868 John Riordon of St. Catharines, using imported machinery, was able to produce ten tons of cheap newsprint a day and other mills soon followed suit. The mass newspaper could not have existed without cheap paper.

While the new machines made the mass production of newspapers possible, they also made it necessary — because they were so expensive. A simple wooden press cost only a few hundred dollars; a newspaper could be founded by almost anyone. But George Brown paid $15,000 for the Hoe Lightning Press he bought in 1867, and the Montreal *Witness* paid twice that for a more advanced model soon after. In 1898 the Montreal *Star* spent $42,000 to acquire fourteen linotypes. Other costs rose as well; more staff was needed to produce the larger newspapers of the early twentieth century, and to distribute them. Only the price of paper fell (from $203 per ton in 1873 to $50 per ton in 1900) as the result of the technological improvements introduced in this period.

Thus a considerable amount of capital was necessary to begin and run a newspaper by the end of the nineteenth century. No longer was the liberal ideal of a multiplicity of newspapers operating as a free marketplace of ideas a reality. Now the rule was that "anything can be said, providing it can be said profitably."[13] By 1900 some Canadian newspapers had assets worth several hundred thousand dollars; they were medium-sized to big businesses, and their proprietors were important Canadian businessmen. As R. S. White of the Montreal *Gazette* summed up the change in 1905:

The character of a newspaper has undergone in the last half century a revolution. Time was ... when the newspaper was owned and directed by one or two gentlemen for the primary purpose of moulding public opinion to a certain cause or causes. The editorial mind was the controlling influence. The business office was of minor consideration, important doubtless on one day of the week — pay day — but a sordid, rather contemptible sort of place for the other five. We have changed all that. To-day the business office dominates seven days of the week, and the editorial mind must be subservient to its necessities. In other words, the newspaper has become a mere commercial enterprise like any other business having as its main purpose the accumulation of wealth.[14]

With rising costs, income had to rise as well, so the competitive push to acquire more and more advertisers by attracting more and more readers accelerated. As the potential audience reached saturation point, papers could grow only by stealing readers from others. Weaker or less cleverly managed papers were forced out of business, and the consolidation and concentration typical of capitalist economies began. By the 1920s the Sifton and Southam families owned newspapers in several cities, beginning a process of building newspaper chains that has continued to this day.

Mass Magazines

Prior to the 1890s, several different kinds of magazines existed in North America, but none of them served a diverse or national readership. Canada produced some of her own literary and intellectual magazines (such as the short lived *Literary Garland, Canadian National Review* and *Le Foyer canadien*), farm and religious periodicals (*Family Herald, Northern Messenger, Messager canadien*), and illustrated magazines (*Canadian Illustrated News, L'Opinion publique illustrée*). In addition, there were magazines serving particular interest groups, like women (*Canadian Home Journal*, founded 1910) or Toronto businessmen and their families (*Saturday Night*, 1887 and *Busy Man's Magazine*, 1896–1911) or university graduates (*Queen's Quarterly, University Magazine*). Especially after the railways were built, élite, special-interest and "sentimental-stories" types of magazines were brought in from the United States as well, for sale either by subscription or on newsstands.

In the 1890s, as a result of the same combination of forces that transformed the newspaper industry, several American magazine publishers fastened on the idea of publishing "middle-of-the-road" national magazines at very low subscription rates. Improved transportation and distribution, expanding technological capabilities, increased literacy and leisure, and the desire of advertisers for access to a larger base of middle-income consumers all played a part in the introduction of these first mass magazines. The best known were Frank Munsey's *Munsey's Magazine*, S.S. McClure's *McClure's*, and Cyrus Curtis's *Saturday Evening Post*. Traditionally, better magazines had cost 25 to 35 cents each; these new periodicals had cover prices of only 10 or 15 cents, and made up the difference with vastly expanded advertising. To appeal to more readers, the editorial content became less serious; most of the articles in these new mass magazines addressed themselves in a very personal way to the interests, hobbies, tastes and problems of the expanding middle class. Like the mass newspapers, these magazines were designed to attract simultaneously a variety of different "publics" within the greater whole; their contents were deliberately diverse, so that each issue would appeal to people with many different interests.[15] The mass magazine caught on almost immediately in the United States, circulations soared and even traditional magazines began to adapt themselves somewhat to the new mode.

In addition to subscriptions mailed through the Post Office, the principal means of distributing these magazines was by newsstand sales. The newsstand distribution business in both the United States and Canada was already by the 1880s monopolized almost totally by the American News Company. Via these two routes American mass magazines came into Canada almost immediately, and the Canadian middle class became as avid readers of the new products as were their American counterparts. One observer claimed that one of the American weekly magazines (probably *Saturday Evening Post*) had a Canadian circulation of 60,000 by 1907 — more than all the major Canadian magazines combined.[16]

Meanwhile, the Canadian magazine industry limped along producing its traditional specialized products with limited circulations and high cover prices. The difficulties to be overcome in order to launch Canadian mass magazines on a national scale were great: the smaller market reduced the economies of scale available, the great distances increased distribution costs, and the lag and external dependency in industrial development meant there were fewer national advertisers looking for outlets. Add to that the competition from the popular, attractive and already easily accessible American magazines, and it is not surprising that it was not until after 1920 that Canadian magazine publishers found it feasible to follow in the footsteps of Munsey, McClure and Curtis.

The most notable Canadian magazine entrepreneur was John Bayne Maclean, who transformed his *Busy Man's Magazine* in 1911 into the general-interest *Maclean's*; he also owned a number of trade publications and special-interest consumer magazines like *Chatelaine*, for women, launched in 1928. By the end of the 1920s *Maclean's* had dropped its cover price substantially and was financed primarily by advertising. Similarly, *Saturday Night* lowered its subscription rates during the 1920s and attempted to broaden its base beyond southern Ontario, as did another older survivor, the *Canadian Magazine*. All of these magazines quite frankly attempted to compete with the popular American periodicals by imitating them. But by then the Canadian magazine market was already overwhelmingly dominated by the U.S., and the Canadian publishers faced an uphill struggle to gain a foothold. In Quebec, although several popular "modern" magazines like *Le Samedi* and *La Revue Populaire* were founded quite early (1889 and 1908 respectively), the mass-consumer magazine did not really take hold until much later, in the 1940s.

By the 1920s Canada possessed a strong and indigenous newspaper industry and a struggling periodical press. All the newspapers and magazines were privately owned, and their revenue was generated primarily from advertising. The media were thus closely linked by both ownership and operation to the business community. It was generally accepted that only a free-enterprise press could be a free press; the notion of government ownership in the information and opinion sector was anathema to virtually everyone. Nevertheless, the government did aid both newspaper and periodical publishers by subsidizing postal rates; it did so in recognition of the important role of the new media in the social and political formation needed to build a new nation. In the 1920s, with the rise of the electronic media and a growing belief that American cultural products competed unfairly in the Canadian marketplace, the government was to be pressed to take an even more active role in media affairs.

The Media and Canadian Nationalism: 1920–1950

Canada's gradual evolution toward complete nationhood, constitutionally, politically and sentimentally, was accelerated by the First World War. The contributions and sacrifices the Dominion made during the war brought pride and convinced many Canadians that the time had come for the country to accept and proclaim its full national status. After a series of imperial conferences, by 1931 Canada was essentially independent of Great Britain. The war also, however, created many challenges for Canada. Regional, class and French-English tensions were exacerbated by wartime conflicts, and the development of the United States to world-power status increased its economic and cultural influence north of the 49th parallel.

In this context, a growing number of concerned English Canadian nationalists struggled in the 1920s to develop a sense of national identity for a divided and disparate population. The "invasion" of Canada by American ideas and values via the mass media became one of their main concerns. In French Canada, conservative nationalists of this era more than ever seemed to be trying to turn their people inward in a defensive search for "la survivance"; they too focussed on the threat of the aggressively material and secular values imported from the United States.

In the 1930s and 1940s these issues were somewhat pushed aside by the more pressing problems of the Great Depression and the Second World War, but the media continued to grow and develop in accordance with Canada's increasingly sophisticated cultural and informational needs. In response to this fact, and particularly with the knowledge that the advent of television was about to transform the media scene even further, in 1948 the Liberal government of Louis St. Laurent appointed a royal commission to study "National Development in the Arts, Letters and Sciences." The Massey (or Massey-Lévesque) Commission examined many subjects besides the mass media, but its comments on this area of Canada's cultural life were a harbinger of a renewed interest in the question of how to reconcile freedom of expression with the national interest in the mass media.

While the print media remained important and influential in the interwar years, the development of cinema and especially the invention of radio broadcasting fundamentally transformed mass communications — and the lives of Canadians. In each of these sectors, national unity, national identity and the threat of Americanization were at issue. The growing strength of the cultural nationalist position was evident in the magazine and broadcasting industries; its failure was most apparent in the movie industry.

Magazines

By the time the First World War ended, hundreds of thousands of middle-class English Canadians were in the habit of purchasing — on the newsstands or by subscription — American mass magazines like *Saturday Evening Post* and *Ladies Home Journal*. By 1925 it was estimated that for every domestic magazine sold in Canada, eight were imported from the United States — a total of around fifty million copies per year.

Canadian magazine publishers entered the competition for readers late, and soon concluded that without drastic action they would likely remain permanently marginal in the Canadian market. The stronger and more aggressive among them decided to fight, in their own self-interest, for a Canadian magazine industry. In 1926, primarily at the instigation of Col. J.B. Maclean, the Magazine Publishers' Association of Canada (MPAC) launched a campaign to persuade the Liberal government to impose a tariff on foreign (by which they meant American) magazines entering Canada.

There was nothing new in this idea — Canadian industries had long used a tariff wall to protect themselves against external competition. From the late nineteenth century on, tariff protection was the umbrella under which Canadian industrialists expanded and prospered. It was a policy that suited manufacturers perfectly, for while aiding them by reducing competition, it preserved the free enterprise system. Thus it is not surprising that the magazine publishers, also facing American competition rooted in economies of scale and prior establishment in the market, turned to the tariff as a remedy.

Tariffs are, of course, highly political, for governments must impose them. In the late 1920s the magazine publishers bombarded the

Liberal government of Mackenzie King with their plea for a tariff. Essentially, their case rested on three grounds, the puritanical, the economic and the nationalist. On the first point, the publishers claimed that many American magazines were salacious and immoral, contributing disproportionately to the corruption of Canadian youth. They argued that no Canadian or British publisher would dream of printing the kind of smutty material that poured in over the border. The government's response, however, was discouraging. If immoral literature was the problem, censorship laws already existed to deal with it — a tariff was not the appropriate instrument to protect the pure minds of young Canadians.

Much more important were the publishers' economic arguments. They pointed out to the government that magazine publishing was a major Canadian industry, employing many thousands of writers, artists, lithographers, printers and so on. If not afforded protection, the industry might collapse, and many would be out of work. This was the traditional economic argument for a tariff; if the government accepted the need for tariffs in the widget industry, why not for magazines? The publishers also made the point that imported magazines carried within them advertising for American manufactured goods, increasing competition for Canadian producers. They reminded the government that flyers containing nothing but advertising were charged a tariff; it seemed anomalous, then, that magazines were allowed in free when many of them were more than half ads.

To these economic arguments there was added a unique twist. Magazine publishing was not just *any* industry, the MPAC asserted. Magazines were the source of information, of ideas, of values and myths. American magazines advertised not only American manufactured goods but the American way of life. If Canada lacked its own magazines, it lacked a vital agency of national communication. *Maclean's* must survive — or the nation would not. Frederick Paul, the editor of *Saturday Night*, put it this way:

Sectionalism is all that now endangers Canadian unity. National periodicals allow people in the different parts of Canada to understand one another's viewpoints, which is the first step towards co-operation and the removal of grievances. If national periodicals are put out of business, New York and Philadelphia become automatically the centers from which all Canadians will draw their information — and opinions ....

> Without the slightest notion of flag-waving or sloppy patriotism, it must be apparent that if we depend on these United States centers for our reading matter we might as well move our government to Washington, for under such conditions it will go there in the end. The press is a stronger cohesive agent than Parliament ....[1]

The publishers' stress on the cultural argument enabled them to rally to their side a number of organizations such as the Canadian Authors' Association which also had both financial and patriotic reasons for fostering the Canadian magazine industry.

It was the misfortune of the magazine publishers and their allies that the Liberals were in power at the time they launched their campaign. The Liberals, traditionally the low-tariff party, in the 1920s were attempting to woo anti-tariff prairie farm voters; they were thus very reluctant to increase tariffs or impose new ones. They were also sensitive to the fact that many ordinary Canadian voters would object to the notion of having to pay more for their favourite American magazines. (The magazine publishers' application was vigorously opposed at Tariff Board hearings by the Consumers' League of Canada and by the American News Company, whose dealers feared loss of sales and revenues.) The King government viewed the publishers' call for a tariff as a purely protectionist demand that would limit competition in order to enrich Canadian publishers at the expense of Canadian consumers.

Additionally, and rather ironically, the very argument used by the magazine publishers, that theirs was a very special industry because it dealt in products for the mind, could also be turned against them. Traditional liberal ideology opposed all restrictions on the free flow of ideas. Canada, small-l liberals argued, would not be threatened but could only benefit and prosper from access to the best ideas and information, wherever they came from. To seal ourselves off from the world by means of this sort of de facto censorship was a sure recipe for national failure. As Mackenzie King declared to the House of Commons:

> Thought is cosmopolitan. It should have no limitation with respect either to place or time. All advances that are made in civilization are the result of ideas, and in any way to preclude the possibility of a good idea having its opportunity of fruition

to the full in any quarter is to retard the progress of civilization itself.[2]

This combination of political and ideological arguments was sufficient to dissuade the Liberals from granting the request for a tariff.

In 1930, however, the unsympathetic Liberals were replaced by R.B. Bennett's Conservatives, who proved to be much more amenable to the imposition of tariffs and to the pleas of publishers who by and large supported them politically. Bennett's government introduced a tariff against imported magazines the following year, calculated according to the amount of advertising material contained (thereby letting in free the "high class" intellectual and cultural magazines). The tariff was specifically justified as compensation for the losses suffered by Canadian manufacturers caused by magazine advertising of American goods. The cover and subscription prices of many of the popular U.S. magazines promptly rose, and their circulations fell by 62 per cent between 1931 and 1935. During the same period Canadian magazines, now more competitive, increased their circulation 64 per cent — and this in the midst of the Great Depression. Some fifty American magazines (for example *True Confessions*, *Argosy*, *Western Romances* and *Battle Aces*) also began printing in Canada the copies intended for Canadian subscribers — exactly the same sort of branch-plant arrangement the tariff had encouraged in other industries.[3] While this did little for Canadian culture or for Canadian authors, it did provide jobs in the printing industry.

The imposition of tariffs against imported magazines was an unprecedented act. Never before had a Canadian government taken upon itself to help a cultural industry by measures designed to discourage the import of foreign products. Prior to the introduction of this tariff in 1931, all governments, whether Liberal or Conservative, had practised an essentially hands-off approach to the print media, whether books, newspapers or magazines. There were only three exceptions to this policy. For a number of years, and particularly during the war, the government had censored or banned material deemed obscene or dangerous. Secondly, indirect aid had been given to the Canadian newspaper industry by the subsidization of the start-up and wireline costs of Canadian Press, the national news cooperative owned by the publishers. Both magazines and newspapers had also been indirectly subsidized by low postal rates for printed material. Otherwise, no government had dared to tread in the dangerous quicksand marked by the banner "Freedom of the Press." The magazine tariff was thus a significant departure.

Yet, it did not prove to be the beginning of a whole new approach to fostering the Canadian media. After five rough Depression years, the Conservatives were thrown out of office in 1935, and in the late 1930s King and the Liberals hastened to sign several major tariff-reducing agreements with the Americans. The duty on magazines was dropped as part of the package. Within three years the value of magazines imported from the U.S. more than doubled. The Canadian magazine industry was left to make it on its own, without aid beyond postal subsidies, until the 1960s and 1970s, when another wave of nationalist concern about American domination of our mass media led to the introduction of other kinds of measures intended to support the indigenous Canadian magazine industry.

The Movie Industry

Simple moving picture cameras and projectors were invented in France and the United States in the late 1880s. The first public movie exhibition in Canada occurred in Montreal in June 1896, featuring several minute-long films using equipment invented by the Lumière brothers. Within months short movies showing one or two scenes of a kiss or a dance became common items in vaudeville theatre programs in the urban centres. Enterprising individuals also put together travelling movie shows which they carried around the countryside.

Movie theatres per se began to be built in the cities after about 1902. The early Nickelodeon theatres provided a program running from twenty minutes to an hour, including several short features such as a travelogue, a comedy and a melodrama, with a lecturer to explain the pictures. In permanent theatres of this type it was of course necessary to change the films frequently. A theatre owner could not possibly afford to buy all the movies needed, so "film exchanges" for renting films were created. These film exchanges were the first movie distributors; they acted as middlemen between the producers of the movies and the owners of the viewing theatres.

By the time the First World War began all Canada's major cities and most of the smaller ones had several movie theatres; there were 830 commercial cinemas nation-wide by 1920. Among the most successful early Canadian theatre entrepreneurs were the Allen brothers, Jules and Jay, who began with the Brantford Theatorium in 1906 and by 1922 had a national chain. For the most part, however, movie-going remained the entertainment of the poorer and less literate elements of the population, especially immigrants, for whom it provided a cheap and accessible way to fill up leisure hours. In 1907 Ernest Ouimet in Montreal built a luxurious cinema, elaborately decorated, with reserved seats and a seven-piece orchestra, in an attempt to woo the middle class to the movies, but his theatre failed and the "respectable classes" did not become regular movie-goers until the 1920s.

During the post-war decade movies became increasingly sophisticated, and so did the advertising and publicity surrounding them. The Hollywood star system and the introduction of "talkies" in 1927 expanded the appeal of movies to all; by the 1930s the cinema was truly a mass medium, at least in the cities. Movie attendance snowballed dramatically in the Depression decade, when the weekly visit to the movie theatre became a popular escapist luxury. By 1936 the average Canadian saw twelve movies per year; by 1950 this number had risen to eighteen. Movie-going hit its peak in Canada in 1952; in that year there were almost 263 million paid admissions. Among other things, this reflected the expansion of suburban movie houses offering two or three double features each week, with cheap Saturday matinées for the children. The "golden age" of movie-going came to a sudden end when television arrived in Canada in 1952.

Before the First World War virtually none of the films shown in Canada were made here. Peter Morris, whose book *Embattled Shadows* is the definitive history of the early Canadian cinema, estimates that 60 per cent of the pre-war movies came from the United States, and the other 40 per cent from Britain and France.[4] He points out that several difficulties slowed the growth of an indigenous movie production industry in Canada: the lack of large urban centres, the absence of native vaudeville, music hall and theatrical traditions, and the shortage of investment capital. Nevertheless, a number of Canadian production companies were formed and Canadian movies were made, especially in the period between 1914 and 1922, when there was considerable demand for patriotic films and newsreels. Regrettably, however, the fact that quite a number of early movie ventures were scams, soured potential investors. In Canada, the movie industry — which by its nature is an expensive business, requiring relatively large and risky investments — has always been preoccupied with a struggle for funding.

The most colourful of the early Canadian movie-makers was undoubtedly Ernest Shipman, an entrepreneur of great panache and nerve (not to mention five wives), who produced seven feature films between 1919 and 1922. Shipman's films were all based on Canadian wilderness tales by popular authors like James Oliver Curwood ("Back to God's Country") and Ralph Connor ("The Man from Glengarry"). They were filmed on location in the Canadian bush, sometimes amidst great difficulties (one star actor caught pneumonia in the minus 45 degree cold at Lesser Slave Lake and died). "Back to God's Country," the first and most successful, featured Shipman's beautiful fourth wife, Nell, and included a brief nude scene. While Shipman's first films were great successes, the later ones were less so, and after a final fiasco with a film called "Blue Water" he left to start over again in Florida.

In large part Shipman's failure was due to a structural change that had occurred by 1923 in the North American movie industry. Initially all movie producers were independent entrepreneurs, finding their own backers, putting the film together, and then negotiating distribution contracts to get the screenings necessary to make the money to pay off the investors. But as films became longer and more complex, and therefore more expensive, investors began to search for ways to reduce their risk. One tactic was the creation of hyperactive publicity campaigns touting highly recognizable stars. A second was vertical integration. By the early 1920s the system of independent producers had been replaced in Hollywood, already the centre of the world's movie industry, by a system dominated by a few large vertically integrated companies that controlled not only production but also distribution and exhibition for their own movies. By this risk-reducing arrangement, largely associated with the genius of Adolph Zukor of Famous Players, the major Hollywood studios were able, within a few years, to squeeze out almost all the independents and so totally dominate the North American movie industry. Theatre-owners could not get popular first-run films to show without cooperating with the majors. The majors insisted that their films fill up most of the available time (a practice known as "block booking"). As a result, independent producers could not get their films distributed or screened. By the Second World War 94 per cent of the total film rental payments in the United States went to the eight Hollywood majors.

This situation affected the Canadian movie industry as much or more than the American. Willing investors were hard enough to come by in Canada without having to risk the consequences of attempting to compete with Famous Players or MGM. In the early 1920s as well, Hollywood began to consider Canada, for accounting purposes, as part of its domestic market, which meant that Canadian and American rights to films were sold as a package. To cap it off, in 1923 Famous Players Canadian Corporation bought out the Allen theatre chain, thus gaining control of the biggest and best movie houses in the largest cities across Canada. Backed by Hollywood capital and with a monopoly on first-run Paramount productions, Famous Players became the most important force in the Canadian movie market. By 1930 all the main motion-picture distributors in Canada were American; they all had to treat Famous Players with kid gloves in order to get their movies into its theatres. A 1930 investigation under the Combines Investigation Act found that Famous Players' vertically integrated ownership pattern was indeed a combine, but legal prosecutors were unable to prove (as the act required) either that this was detrimental to the public interest or that competition was lessened unduly, so the accused companies were acquitted.[5] The move toward concentration of ownership of theatres continued during the 1930s and accelerated during the Second World War. By 1945 chains owning twenty or more theatres, mainly foreign-owned, collected 60 per cent of the total admission receipts in Canada.

The combination of all these factors meant that after about 1923 a feature film industry virtually ceased to exist in Canada. The Canadians (both English- and French-speaking) who flocked to the movies in the 1930s and 1940s saw almost entirely American films. Even the movies about Canada were Hollywood-made, perpetuating the stereotypes of a wilderness country inhabited by treacherous Indians, sly half-breeds, uncouth French-Canadian trappers and, of course, beautiful maidens rescued from horrible fates by stalwart Mounties.[6] "Rose Marie," starring Jeannette MacDonald and Nelson Eddy, is only the best known of a large number of such screen gems. In 1953, at the peak of Canadian movie-going, 74.6 per cent of the 1,289 feature films put into circulation came from the United States, 16.9 per cent from France, 5.8 per cent from Britain, 1.2 per cent from Italy, 1.1 per cent from other foreign countries, and 0.1 per cent from Canada. Newsreels as well were largely imported from the U.S., with small Canadian segments added.

Where was the government during all this? In fact, both provincial and federal levels of government got involved in movies at a fairly early stage. By 1915 eight provinces had set up censorship boards to screen all movies for immoral and unpatriotic scenes. These boards, which continue to exist to this day, were much more active and intrusive in their censorship than was ever the case with printed materials. The Quebec Bureau de Surveillance, for example (and it was typical), in 1922–3 prohibited among many other things any scenes showing rape, adultery, free love, "close-up views of bathing girls in one-piece suits," burglaries, thefts, forgeries, cheating at cards, cruelty, violence to women and children, brutality to animals, divorce, suicide, and "all scenes injurious to Canadian ... patriotism and to the loyalty to the king."[7] A strong class-bias was apparent; the principle of freedom of expression was never as sacred for a medium whose audience was assumed to be less rational and more impressionable than that which consumed the printed word. (Nowadays the boards function mainly to protect youth by classifying films as well as videos and CD-ROMs with respect to their age-appropriateness. Quebec still refuses classification for films that "promote or condone sexual violence.")[8]

In addition, several provinces, and the federal government as well, set up their own cinema offices to make films to attract tourists and immigrants and for educational purposes. The most active of the government film bureaus, the Ontario Motion Picture Bureau and the federal Exhibits and Publicity Bureau (later renamed the Canadian Government Motion Picture Bureau), were formed in 1917 and 1918 respectively. No attempt was made, however, to make feature (full-length story) films or to give financial aid to private Canadian companies that wished to do so. Indeed, it was the oft-stated belief of Ray Peck, for many years the head of the federal bureau, that Canada could gain nothing by attempting to compete with the Americans in feature films. We should simply accept that the Americans were the best in the world in that genre, he argued, and concentrate instead on more utilitarian scenic travelogues. Among the films produced by the Canadian government under his leadership were such blockbusters as "The Apples of Annapolis" and "Where Snow-Time is Joy-Time."

Canada was not alone in facing heavy American competition in the movie industry. Many European countries, with their nascent domestic film industries devastated by the First World War, confronted the same challenge in the 1920s. The difference was that most of them instituted protective measures to rectify the situation. The most common device was some sort of quota on screenings. For example, after a 1926 investigation showed that only 5 per cent of the movies shown in Britain were of British origin, Parliament in London passed legislation requiring a quota of 20 per cent British films. The definition of British, however, was expanded (partly on the urging of the Canadians at the 1926 Imperial Conference) to include all films produced anywhere in the Commonwealth.

The Canadian government took no similar action. Two attempts to introduce quotas at the provincial level were apparently aborted by intensive lobbying by the American-dominated Motion Picture Exhibitors and Distributors of Canada.[9] In fact, at the urging of Motion Picture Bureau chief Peck, the federal government followed quite a different tack. In 1927 Peck paid a two-month visit to Hollywood explicitly to encourage American studios to establish branch plants in Canada to circumvent the British quota. "We invite Americans to come over to Canada to make automobiles and a thousand and one other things," he wrote, "and why not invite them to come over and make pictures ...?"[10] Instead of taking advantage of the British law to develop a Canadian film industry, or even more to the point, instead of passing similar quota legislation (as Australia did), the official Canadian approach was to bolster the Hollywood monopoly of the North American film industry.

Hollywood accepted the handout. A number of studios set up branch operations, mostly in Victoria. In the next decade over twenty films were produced in Canada for the British market — virtually the entire Canadian output of these years. These films (the so-called "quota quickies") were despised and deplored by British officials; in 1938 the British revised their law to exclude Commonwealth films, largely because of the Canadian contravention of its spirit. The Hollywood studios promptly packed up and went home.

Similar shortsightedness on the part of the Canadian government was apparent in the late 1940s. Desperately short of gold and American dollars by 1947, the federal government imposed a variety of restrictions on luxury imports from the United States in order to improve Canada's balance of trade. Despite predictions that the measures would include a quota system to force Hollywood to reinvest at least some of its Canadian profits in local film-making, the movie industry was left untouched. Instead, Canadian officials bought what Pierre Berton in *Hollywood's Canada* has succinctly described as a "public relations man's boondoggle," the Canadian Co-operation Project. This was a scheme whereby Hollywood movies were injected with scraps of Canadian content ostensibly to encourage American tourists to add Canada to their itineraries. Thus, for example, in a movie entitled "New York Confidential," a script that had previously read "They caught Louis Engleday in Detroit" was changed to read "They caught Louis Engleday on his way to Canada." Berton is particularly scathing about the line James Stewart was given in "Bend of the River": "Those are red-wing orioles from Canada." Like Canadian feature films, there was no such thing.[11] In 1947 $6 million left Canada to pay for rentals of American films; by 1973 the figure had multiplied more than six times to almost $40 million.

The federal government did make one positive contribution to the film industry. In 1938, it invited a Scottish documentary filmmaker named John Grierson to survey and report on Canadian government film production and distribution. The result was the passage of the 1939 National Film Act, setting up the National Film Board (NFB) as a liaison and review agency to coordinate film production by government departments and by the Government Motion Picture Bureau. The National Film Board's first head was, of course, the dynamic John Grierson. In 1941 the NFB absorbed the Motion Picture Bureau and began not only to advise and coordinate but to produce films and distribute them.

All of this occurred within the context of a great spurt in government filmmaking for wartime propaganda. Under Grierson's leadership, the NFB produced for both national and international distribution a large number of highly regarded short films and documentaries, both on war-related topics and others. Most notable perhaps were the two propaganda series, "World in Action" and "Canada Carries On." By the late 1940s the NFB studios were coming to be known as world-class centres of experimentation with animation techniques as well. But the NFB rarely produced feature films. It has been argued by at least one film historian, in fact, that Grierson agreed with earlier heads of Canadian government film bureaus that feature films were best left to Hollywood.[12] This view was rooted in part in a deep belief in the documentary as a means of portraying and confronting real life as opposed to the conventional use of film as an entertaining avenue of escape from reality. It may also have been a product of Grierson's desire to maintain good relations with the American distribution companies which determined the fate of his films and of his faith in internationalism and multinationals.[13] Considerations of the enormous cost of producing feature films may have been involved as well. Whatever the reason for the NFB's decision virtually to ignore feature-film production, the result was that the movie industry in Canada had in effect two separate parts by 1950: a private sector that imported commercial features largely from the United States and a public sector that made and distributed "serious" and Canadian documentary films. The former was the mainstream; the latter was marginal.

Radio Broadcasting

Radio broadcasting began shortly after the First World War almost by accident, as a new use of a technology that had been perfected years earlier for the transmission of business and military information. Up to the end of the First World War it was assumed by all involved that radio would serve a purpose similar to that of the telegraph and telephone: to send messages from one individual to another. Only after the war, as various electrical companies sought customers for the equipment they had the surplus capacity to manufacture, did they stumble upon the notion of deliberately transmitting information and entertainment to large numbers of anonymous individuals simultaneously. This concept of "broadcasting" emerged almost at the same time in various countries. Most notably, it was developed by the Westinghouse Company in Pittsburgh, where KDKA (usually credited with being the first American station) began regular broadcasting in November 1920, and by the Marconi Company in Montreal, which had its experimental station XWA (later CFCF) on the air at about the same time.

A large number of others soon leapt on the bandwagon. By 1923 Canada had over thirty stations in operation, by 1930 over sixty. Businesses usually became involved in broadcasting as an adjunct to their other activities; many of the early Canadian stations were owned by electrical retailers or by newspapers. In the United States broadcasting developed even more rapidly, in large part because the huge electrical manufacturing companies (Westinghouse, General Electric and RCA) poured enormous sums of money into erecting technically sophisticated high-power stations to stimulate the sale of the radio receivers they produced. While these corporations had manufacturing subsidiaries in Canada (to leap the tariff barrier) they made little attempt to establish broadcasting stations here. Canada's early broadcasting industry was collectively weakened by the fact that there were no equally large Canadian corporations here interested in financing the perfection of the science and the art. Instead Canadian broadcasting remained until almost the end of the 1920s the preserve of smaller businesses with other interests and little capital. By that time advertising revenue had become the main source of income for the broadcasting stations of both countries.[14]

Radio rapidly evolved from being a novelty to a household necessity. By 1931 one-third of Canadians had radios, and a larger proportion in the cities. By 1940 three-quarters of all Canadian homes had radios and by 1950 almost all. From the beginning, Canadians listened in large numbers to the best and most powerful American stations. Their signals carried freely over the border, for there was little interference from Canadian stations or other electrical devices. As with mass magazines and movies, Canadians, especially English-speaking Canadians, became habituated to American popular culture, its trends, tastes and stars, on this new medium.

The real crunch began in 1927, with the formation of the two American networks, NBC and CBS. The network arrangement allowed stations across the country to share programming, thereby reducing the per-unit cost and enabling the hiring of the most talented writers, singers and orchestras. While somewhat makeshift Canadian network arrangements also existed, including a chain of stations owned and operated by the Canadian National Railway, the popularity in Canada of the best American programming and the consequent eagerness of advertisers to sponsor it made joining an American network economically attractive to several of the largest urban Canadian stations. By 1930 CFRB Toronto and CKAC Montreal had joined the CBS network and CKGW Toronto and CFCF Montreal had joined NBC. To the middle-class nationalist élite it seemed that yet another Canadian mass medium was about to become dominated by the United States. Indeed, the comparison with the movie industry was made explicitly by individuals such as Charles Bowman, editor of the Ottawa *Citizen*, and the cry went out for direct government intervention to prevent broadcasting from suffering the fate of the erstwhile Canadian film industry.

Radio was unlike the other media discussed so far in one extremely important respect. From the beginning (in the Canadian case 1905, long before broadcasting was even dreamt of) it was regulated by the government. In Canada the regulatory authority was the federal Department of Marine and Fisheries, because of radio's early use as a marine navigational aid. Government regulation was deemed necessary for two main reasons. The first was primarily a matter of national security: the authorities feared the use of radio-transmitting equipment for surreptitious purposes; accordingly they imposed a requirement that all radio equipment must be licensed. This included both transmitters and receivers; until 1953 all Canadians who owned radio sets were required to purchase a licence annually. Secondly, there was only a limited number of frequencies available for radio use, and unacceptable interference occurred unless someone enforced the allocation of wavelengths or frequencies to the various parties. The issue of wavelength allocation became of even greater concern once the broadcasting era began because the acquisition of a licence to use one of the relatively scarce frequencies eventually became a considerable privilege. It bears repeating, however, that throughout the first formative decade of Canadian broadcasting, while there was government regulation, the broadcasting stations themselves were virtually all privately owned and run for profit, and that there was almost no regulation of program content. Regulation existed for technical, not cultural, reasons.

A combination of regulatory and economic difficulties and the spread of the American networks prompted the King government to set up a royal commission on radio broadcasting in 1928. This was but the first of many such inquiries into Canada's mass media. The Aird Commission, as it was called after its chairman, Sir John Aird, issued its report in 1929. The commissioners unanimously recommended that Canadian broadcasting be completely taken over by the government and that a Canadian Radio Broadcasting Commission be set up modelled along the lines of the British Broadcasting Corporation (BBC) in Great Britain. The proposed commission was to take possession of all existing facilities and to construct a chain of seven powerful stations to provide coast-to-coast service. With the help of provincial advisory committees, it was also to produce all programming, although the commissioners were vaguer on that aspect. It was to be financed by the receiving licence fees and by advertising.

Needless to say, the report stirred up a controversy. It would not be incorrect to say that the debate over the proposal to nationalize radio was the first time Canadians collectively and Parliament in particular ever confronted and discussed in depth such questions as: Who should own the mass media? Who should control them? How should they be financed? Is it important that Canada have its own mass media? The Liberal government fell before taking any action, and it was left to Bennett and the Conservatives to decide what to do. Finally, in the spring of 1932, a Radio Broadcasting Act was passed that did indeed create a government-owned Canadian Radio Broadcasting Commission (CRBC), but that also allowed for the continued existence of privately owned stations. The commission was also given the task of regulating all broadcasting.

The CRBC was severely hampered from the beginning by faulty organization and lack of funds. The result was that it was unable to build the stations needed to create a national network. In order to fulfil its mandate to provide radio service to all Canadians, the CRBC was forced to purchase time on major private stations, thereby delaying (permanently, it turned out) the conversion of the private stations into purely supplementary services. The managerial problems of the CRBC resulted in its reorganization into the Canadian Broadcasting Corporation (CBC) in 1936. The pattern had already been set, however. Due to lack of political will, the wholly government-owned broadcasting system recommended by the Aird Commission never came into being.

The 1940s and early 1950s were the "golden age" of Canadian radio, especially on the CBC. The mass demand for war news bolstered the CBC's news and information programming, and its audience. The corporation also offered a wide range of serious and light entertainment such as "The Happy Gang," "CBC Stage" and of course "Hockey Night in Canada." Powerful regional transmitters were set up on the prairies and in the maritimes, consolidating and bolstering the network audience. Between 1944 and 1962 the CBC even set up a second network to provide lighter fare for mass audiences. But the private stations were allowed to grow alongside, serving local advertisers and audiences. According to the official view, Canadian radio was a "single system" comprising CBC-owned and -operated stations, privately owned stations affiliated with the CBC networks, and independent private stations — all regulated by the CBC's Board of Governors. In fact, what gradually began to occur was a separation into two systems, one consisting of the CBC and the other the private broadcasters, who by the late 1940s were loudly criticizing the CBC as "at one and the same time competitor, regulator, prosecutor, jury and judge."[15] The growing strength and wealth of the private broadcasters in the 1940s and 1950s made it increasingly clear that Canada did not have a "single" but a "mixed" broadcasting system, in which the CBC network, financed by parliamentary grants and advertising revenues, co-existed with a private sector of locally-oriented stations, financed solely by ad income. Throughout this period Canadians continued to have easy access to American radio programs by direct reception and via both the public and private Canadian stations. A detailed analysis conducted in 1949 showed that about 20 per cent of the CBC's main Trans-Canada Network's programs were of American origin, mostly drama and variety.[16] Three Canadian stations remained linked to American networks: CFRB Toronto, CKAC Montreal and CKWX Vancouver.

A comparison between broadcasting and the other mass media discussed so far is of some interest. Why was it that in the case of broadcasting the Canadian government was moved to break (at least partially) from the common North American pattern of private ownership of the mass media? While it was demonstrable that the much larger size and economic clout of the United States, its world leadership in popular culture, as well as a shared language and geographic contiguity, had made existence difficult if not impossible for both the Canadian magazine industry and the Canadian feature film industry, the Canadian government had done almost nothing to aid either. Then suddenly in 1932, in a third medium, broadcasting, it embarked on the project of owning its own stations, running its own networks and producing most of the programming for both. Why?

The most obvious explanation, which Prime Minister Bennett himself offered, was that the government was convinced that broadcasting was a very special industry in its ability to facilitate nationwide inter-communication. While newspapers were local, magazines middle-class and movies purely entertainment, radio appealed to all classes, in all parts of the country, and could be successfully used not only for entertainment but for informational and propaganda purposes. A public broadcasting company, Bennett believed, could be the longed-for twentieth-century equivalent to the CPR, utilizing the latest communications technology to unite and bind the nation. Thus, like the railway, radio was a special case, necessitating government involvement beyond the normal North American notion of the state's role in economic or cultural matters. American domination of radio was simply not acceptable. (It should be noted that in most other parts of the world government ownership of radio was taken as a matter of course from the very beginning.)

Bennett was a free-enterpriser but he was also a Canadian nationalist. He may be described as a member of the Canadian commercial élite whose banking and transportation interests lay in the survival of the east-west connection. Once he became convinced (at least in part through the effective lobbying of a small group called the Canadian Radio League) that the existing system of private radio would almost inevitably lead to the Americanization of a crucial cultural industry, he became an advocate of public broadcasting. Of all Canada's mass media, broadcasting remains the only one whose problems have been addressed by means of substantial government ownership.

The French Language Media

While much of what has been said about magazines, films and radio in the period between 1920 and 1950 applies equally to English- and French-language media, there were certain special features of the Quebec situation that deserve brief note. Most important, Quebec's distinctive language both encouraged more indigenous cultural development and offered some protection from the tidal wave of American popular culture pouring into Canada in these years. By the Second World War, for example, both private French radio stations and the separate Radio-Canada French network set up by the CBC in 1938 produced many popular, locally based dramatic serials.[17] In English Canada, in contrast, the CBC produced more serious drama and the private broadcasters almost no drama at all. English-Canadian radio relied on imports of U.S. soap operas and mystery series for popular dramatic programming.

Because the language provided the native culture a certain "natural" protection vis-à-vis radio, newspapers and periodicals, Quebec's middle-class nationalist élite focussed mainly on the threat of the cinema. The most worried were the conservative, clerically inspired nationalists, who viewed the movies as the prime exemplar of the moral decadence of modern, urban North America so threatening to the survival of the French Canadian family and nation. Despite considerable agitation from this group against the "Jewish-American" film industry,[18] they were notably unsuccessful in persuading the Quebec government to enact restrictive policies until the tragic 1927 Laurier Palace fire in Montreal in which seventy-eight children died, when a ban on child attendance at movies was imposed. Otherwise, however, not only were Quebec's movie attendance rates as high as anywhere else in Canada, but Quebec was the first, and for a long time the only, province to allow Sunday movies. As in English Canada, the concerns of the nationalist élite and the actions of the people were not always congruent.

The Massey Commission

The idea of a royal commission to investigate Canadian arts, letters and sciences was promoted in the late 1940s by a group of concerned civil servants and Liberals, among them Brooke Claxton, Jack Pickersgill and Lester Pearson. They sold the idea to Louis St. Laurent after he became prime minister, and the five-person commission headed by long-time cultural nationalist Vincent Massey was created in 1949. The commissioners began, in their own words, with the twin assumptions that "there are important things in the life of a nation which cannot be weighed or measured" and that national traditions and national unity exist not only in the material sphere but in the "realm of ideas."[19] Given such assumptions, it is not surprising that much of the report and many of its recommendations were taken up with an examination of Canada's "high" culture: universities, research, libraries, museums, ballet, art and so on. In these areas, the commissioners were relatively optimistic that with determination, organization and money, much could be accomplished.

A key section of the Massey Report also dealt with the mass media, and here the commissioners indulged in considerable handwringing. On the one hand, their nationalist and élitist views of Canadian culture led them to deplore the fact that so much of what Canadians read, heard and saw came from an "alien source." On the other hand, they were sensitive to the principle of freedom of expression and to the clear evidence that ordinary Canadians enjoyed and appreciated the products of the American mass media. In the end, they came down firmly on the side of cultural nationalism. Their recommendations regarding the mass media included a total rejection of the "industrial" view presented by private broadcasters. To the commissioners, working from liberal humanist nationalist principles, broadcasting was clearly "a public trust" and "a public service."[20] Accordingly they recommended the retention of the power and privileges of the CBC in the radio field and a clean and clear head start for the CBC in television, just then appearing on the horizon. At bottom, the commissioners accepted the slogan coined by Graham Spry of the Canadian Radio League twenty years earlier: "The State or the United States." The only means of preventing the Americanization of Canada's media was at least partial government ownership; a purely commercial system would inevitably be an American one.

The Massey Commission's firm belief in the CBC as the saviour of the Canadian "national tradition" was a culmination of thirty years of debate among the nationalist élite about the role of the mass media in Canada. But economic, technological and social forces continued to shape the Canadian media as well, usually in the opposite direction. In the fifty years since the Massey Report the tensions among the various parties have multiplied as the stakes have grown.

The Television Age

Television was the pre-eminent mass medium of the last half of the twentieth century. While the structure of the industry changed considerably in the 1980s and 1990s, TV will certainly remain a central component of mass communications for the foreseeable future. All the previously existing mass media, including radio, films, newspapers and magazines, were affected by the rise of television, some more than others. Both the roles and the revenues of the other cultural industries were challenged by the arrival of this dynamic new competitor.

Television

The technology enabling the wireless transmission of pictures was developed in Britain in the late 1920s; experimentation continued in the 1930s in a number of centres, including (briefly) the École Polytechnique in Montreal. Early broadcasting in Britain and the United States was halted by the onset of the Second World War. When work toward commercial use of television recommenced at the end of the war progress came quickly. Twenty-four stations were licensed in the U.S. in 1946 and over one hundred by 1948. By 1949 almost a million Americans owned TV sets, or 2.3 per cent of all households; by 1951 those numbers had jumped to 10.3 million and 23.5 per cent. Unlike radio, television signals do not follow the earth's curvature, so transmission distances are much more limited. Nevertheless, Canadians living close to U.S. stations were able, with the help of high antennas, to receive American television early. By 1949 there were at least 3,600 television sets in Canada, but no Canadian TV stations.

That year the federal government outlined an interim policy for television development by both public and private enterprise. According to this plan, the CBC's Board of Governors was to be responsible for general policy, for the licensing of both CBC and private stations, and for all network arrangements. CBC production centres were to be set up in Toronto and Montreal and stations were to be opened in those two cities immediately, followed later by expansion to other parts of the country.

After three years of hurried labour, the first two CBC TV stations, CBFT Montreal and CBLT Toronto, began broadcasting in the fall of 1952. But extending the network to the east and west promised to be extremely expensive. Not only were there heavy capital costs for the construction of new stations and network links, but over the long term programming and transmission expenses up to six or seven times those of radio had to be anticipated. While the government did substantially increase its funding to the CBC, and provide it for a time with the revenue from a new 15 per cent tax on the sale of TV sets, building the complete network immediately was deemed financially impossible. Lacking the funds to erect a full network of stations, the CBC therefore entered into an arrangement that paralleled the way its radio network had operated since the 1930s: while a few more CBC owned- and operated-stations were built in the next few years, in many smaller centres privately owned stations were licensed with the proviso that they carry the full basic CBC network service. For the time being and in the interests of equity, no competition was allowed; each market area could have only one station until most of the country had some service.

The new medium spread extremely rapidly. By 1960 there were forty-seven stations in Canada, nine CBC and the rest privately owned CBC affiliates; they were linked together by a costly ($50-million) coast-to-coast microwave relay system. The CBC's operating and capital budget exceeded $100 million a year by the end of the decade. Only those Canadians living in the most remote areas were beyond the range of a Canadian TV station by 1960, and three-quarters of all homes possessed a television set. Those sets were turned on an average of six hours a day. In less than a decade, television had become the number one in-home leisure activity of Canadians.

Despite these great and expensive accomplishments, many Canadians were dissatisfied with the system in place at the end of the 1950s. About one-quarter of the population, mainly those in southern Ontario, Quebec and British Columbia, were within range of American TV stations, and had access not only to the programs offered on the CBC but to those on the major American networks as well. Meanwhile, viewers in the rest of the country felt aggrieved; because of the government's monopoly policy, their only choice was to tune in to the CBC or not. Such a situation could not last. In 1958 the Conservative government of John Diefenbaker announced that it would allow competitive stations; within a couple of years eight licences were granted to private groups to set up second stations in the larger cities in competition with CBC-owned or -affiliated ones. After a few complicated manoeuvres, a second network, CTV, was authorized that acted as an agency through which the individual private stations could share programs. By 1963 CTV had its own microwave relay system linking its affiliates from coast to coast. In 1961 Télémetropole was licensed to provide a private French-language station in the large Montreal market as well. (In 1971 this station became the anchor of the private French network, Télé-Diffuseurs Associés or TVA.)

The Diefenbaker Conservatives also made another momentous decision in 1958. After years of complaints from private broadcasters that they should not be regulated by their competitor, the CBC, a new Broadcasting Act was passed creating an independent regulatory body, the Board of Broadcast Governors (BBG) to which both the CBC and the private stations (radio and television) were responsible. It was thus the BBG that licensed what became the CTV network stations and that set and enforced the standards all Canadian broadcasters were henceforth to meet.

Perhaps the most important and certainly the most controversial of those standards concerned the amount of foreign (read American) programming Canadian television stations were allowed to schedule. From its earliest days, the CBC television network (like CBC radio before it) purchased certain popular American shows, many of which were shown to appreciative audiences in prime time. There were a couple of justifications for this policy. Making good television shows was and is a very expensive proposition. Popular programs could be bought from the American networks (which had already recovered their costs in their own large market) for a fraction of the expenditure involved in producing them in Canada. Because the shows were usually well-made, heavily promoted and attuned to mass tastes, their Canadian audiences were large and therefore so were the ad revenues they produced. While the CBC received government funding, it still desperately needed that ad revenue, which helped "cross-subsidize" the production of Canadian programs. Besides, those Canadians outside the range of American stations would have been even more infuriated with the lack of multiple local TV stations in the 1950s if the CBC had denied them "I Love Lucy" or "The Jackie Gleason Show."

Once private stations began operations, they, too, began importing popular American shows. But because their *raison d'être* was profit maximization and they had no government subsidies, they were inclined to import a much higher proportion of inexpensive American material and to produce less of their own. Critic Robert Fulford called CTV the "anti-network" — it was simply "a distributor of programmes from elsewhere," he contended.[1] Dramatic programs were most frequently imported, because skill, experience and money had made the Americans world leaders in the production of polished and professional sitcoms and crime serials that were, the ratings showed, as popular with English Canadian audiences as with American. In its struggle to compete with the CTV stations in the major markets, and to keep its privately owned affiliates happy, the CBC in turn was tempted to offer more and more American programs.

Thus before each season began, executives from the two Canadian networks hastened to Hollywood to purchase what they anticipated would be the most popular American series to fill their prime time slots. Home-grown programming more and more was confined to sports, news and public affairs and to non-peak hours, except on the French stations, which were able partly as a result of the protection afforded by language differences to continue the Quebec radio tradition of producing indigenous popular dramatic-serial type programs (*téléromans*).

This situation was viewed with alarm by a considerable number of English Canadians, including nationalist intellectuals, actors and others seeking employment, and the management of the CBC, which was faced with the impossible task of fulfilling the corporation's mandate to create and transmit Canadian culture while at the same time competing for ad revenue with private stations that imported bargain-priced Hollywood shows. These groups were particularly concerned about the lack of Canadian-made entertainment programming, because they were convinced of the cultural importance of drama and other entertainment formats. In 1960 the Board of Broadcast Governors, in response to these criticisms, introduced Canadian content guidelines to which all television stations had to adhere. Fifty-five per cent (later raised to 60 per cent) of all programs broadcast were to be of Canadian origin, although the definition of "Canadian" was generous.[2]

A number of difficulties ensued. The private stations in many cases responded by creating cheap game shows which they ran in morning time slots, leaving the lucrative prime-time schedule packed with imported sitcoms. A study done in 1965 revealed that while the average CBC-owned station in a major city devoted 57 per cent of its evening schedule to Canadian produced programs, the average "second station" (privately owned) gave only 34 per cent of its evening hours to Canadian shows. The Fowler Committee, one of numerous bodies asked to investigate Canadian broadcasting in the last thirty years, concluded in 1965:

> The advent of private Canadian stations in areas where the CBC formerly provided the only service might have been expected to increase the availability of programs of Canadian origin. In fact ... it worked in the opposite direction.[3]

Although regulations were later amended to impose percentage quotas on prime time as well, these also were easily evaded. The simple fact is that it was (and is) not in the economic interest of the private broadcasters to produce shows domestically when imports cost less and earn more. To put it another way, with two coast-to-coast networks completed by 1963, Canada's television distribution capacity had expanded more quickly than the ability (or funding) to provide it with home-grown programs.

Since the mid 1960s, many of the trends evident in the first decade of Canadian television have been consolidated, but the industry has also become very much more complex. Over-the-air there are now four national networks (CBC, Radio-Canada, CTV and CanWest Global), regional television-station groupings like CHUM and Télémetropole, a number of privately owned independent stations, provincial educational stations, and a northern network. In addition, of course, there are now many specialty and pay-TV channels available on cable and by satellite. All are regulated under the provisions of an updated Broadcasting Act passed in 1991 and by an updated regulatory body, the Canadian Radio-television and Telecommunications Commission (CRTC).

Within this mix, the original dominance of the CBC in Canadian television has been sharply reduced. CBC English-language stations now are watched by less than 10 per cent of the English-speaking audience, and, whether as cause or effect, the CBC's parliamentary allocations have been regularly cut back. In 1932 the Canadian government decided to make the publicly owned CBC the central component of the broadcasting system, and that was confirmed by the way television was initially developed. Nearly seventy years later, the public sector is an increasingly marginal part of a broadcasting system dominated by private business.

Television remains by far the most popular home-leisure activity. Ninety-seven per cent of Canadians live in a household with at least one television set; well over half have two or more. In 1998, Canadians watched an average of 22.3 hours of television a week (down from 24.5 in 1995). Women, especially Francophone Québécois and Maritime women, are the heaviest viewers.

Television remains primarily an entertainment medium. In 1997, about 62 per cent of the shows watched by Anglophones were dramas, comedy, variety, music, games or sports, and the figure for Francophones was only slightly less at 60.8 per cent.[4] In English Canada, 70 per cent of audience viewing time in 1997 was spent watching foreign (mainly American) programs, although this was a noticeable drop from over 80 per cent in 1984–5. Only 12 per cent of the drama programs watched by Anglophones were Canadian, but 72 per cent of the news and public affairs programs were domestically produced. Canadian drama remains the second-smallest audience viewing category on the English-language networks; only Canadian comedy ranks lower. Averaging the fall 1998/spring 1999 sweeps periods, the top ten shows in Canada were, in order: "ER," "Friends," "Frasier," "Wheel of Fortune," "Ally McBeal," "The X-Files," "Jeopardy," "Hockey Night in Canada," "Jesse," and "Sixty Minutes." Of these, four are seen in Canada on the CTV network, five on Global, and one (hockey, of course) on CBC.[5] The comment of the 1986 Task Force on Canadian Broadcasting headed by Gerald Caplan and Florian Sauvageau remains apt: "English Canadians ... are virtual strangers in television's land of imagination."[6] The situation in French-language television is somewhat different. According to 1997 figures, 66.5 per cent of all French-language viewing was of Canadian programming. Moreover (and indicating a large drop from the 1980s), less than 50 per cent of drama programs viewed on French-language TV stations were foreign.

The most significant change in television since the 1960s (aside from the introduction of colour in 1966) is the proliferation of channels. Not only are there more Canadian stations and networks, but American channels have become available to millions more Canadians via cable and to a lesser extent by satellite dish receivers. At least

75 per cent of Canadian homes had at least one cable connection in 1999, and a much higher proportion in some localities (for example over 90 per cent in Vancouver). Canada is one of the most-cabled countries in the world. The combination of cable and satellite distribution has also enabled the introduction of a large number of specialty and pay-TV channels, both Canadian and (on a restricted basis) American.

The proliferation of stations and of cable and satellite dishes has had a double consequence: while each customer has an expanded amount of station choice, the total audience is fragmented, which somewhat reduces its attractiveness to advertisers. The viewing of Canadian programs is also reduced in cabled homes. In 1986, for example, in households which received television only off-air, 29 per cent of the viewing was of Canadian programs. For those with cable this dropped to 22 per cent. In both cases the proportion of viewing approximately equalled the proportional availability of Canadian programs.

The effect of pay and specialty channels on viewing habits has been particularly marked in the last fifteen years. According to figures produced for the Friends of Canadian Broadcasting, looking at English-language stations only, CBC, CTV and Global among them had 55 per cent of the viewing share in 1984–5, pay/specialty channels slightly less than 2 per cent, other Canadian stations 11 per cent and American stations 32 per cent. By 1990–1, the three networks had dropped to 45 per cent (Global gained, while CBC and CTV both lost share), pay/specialty channels had increased to almost 13 per cent, other Canadian stations to 14 per cent, and the share of American stations had dropped to 28.5 per cent.[7] The estimates for the year 2000 suggest that the Canadian over-the-air networks will attract about 52 per cent of the audience, specialty channels (both Canadian and American) about 35 per cent, and most of the other American networks 13 per cent.[8] While television is and will remain a central element in the media mix, the changes resulting from channel abundance have already been significant, and the future seems to promise that the trend toward fragmentation will continue and perhaps accelerate.

Radio

The rapid rise of television affected the previously established mass media in differing ways. The most immediate and drastic effect was on radio. Within a handful of years network radio ceased to exist in the United States, although it did survive in altered form in Canada on the CBC. National advertisers moved en bloc to television; so did virtually all dramatic and public affairs programming, as well of course as did many of the executives, producers, announcers, actors, musicians and technicians who had staffed the radio networks. With the exception of the truncated CBC radio network, radio in Canada as in the U.S. became a purely local service, catering to local listeners and to local advertisers. No longer did people listen to the radio in the evening; now "prime time" was between 7 and 9 in the morning and to a lesser extent 4 and 6 in the afternoon. (The tendency to peak listening in the "drive" times was accelerated by the rise in commuting in the same era; one-third of all radio listening now occurs in vehicles.)

With television the new "mass" medium, radio stations began to specialize more, tailoring their programming to particular audience tastes. In the late 1950s and 1960s many stations began concentrating on particular musical formats such as top 40, MOR (middle-of-the-road), country and western, or rock, anchored by disk jockeys. In the 1970s and 1980s, much of the popular music programming moved to the FM band, and AM stations began to offer more eclectic mixes of open-line phone-in shows, news, sports and music. CBC radio virtually abandoned the battle for big ratings and offered more serious programming (a mixture of local and national shows, commercial-free after 1975) that attracted small but dedicated audiences (a less-than-10 per cent market share). There are also a number of community, educational and aboriginal radio stations providing an alternative voice.

Although radio has changed a great deal in the last forty years, it is still one of the most widespread and widely utilized media. There are more than 900 radio stations in Canada, the vast majority of them privately owned and almost totally dependent on advertising income. Ninety-eight per cent of Canadians can receive AM radio stations, and 85 per cent FM. The average Canadian listens to radio twenty-one hours a week; residents of Quebec and women over thirty-five are disproportionately heavy radio listeners. Very few listen to American stations. In order to encourage the Canadian music industry, the CRTC in 1971 and 1975 introduced Canadian-content rules for the records played on Canadian radio stations. On AM radio stations, 35 per cent of the musical content must now be Canadian, while the rules for FM vary depending on the format of the station. The definition of "Canadian" for the purpose of this regulation is that any two of four aspects of the music be Canadian: the composer, the lyricist, the performer, or the performance or recording process. It is also required that 65 per cent of the vocals on French-language radio stations be in French. Canadian radio stations are also obliged by the CRTC to carry news broadcasts.

In the last thirty years radio has received a relatively steady ten or eleven per cent of the total amount spent on media advertising. Recently, however, television has been attracting more local advertising, and cutting into radio revenues. Many AM stations were in financial difficulties in the early 1990s, so in 1998 the CRTC began to allow more multiple-station ownership in the same market in order to improve profitability and stability. More and more radio stations are also beginning to use satellite connections to provide network or syndicated programming, especially for sports, news and what the CRTC calls "foreground" material. A fair proportion of this material, such as the ubiquitous "Dr. Laura," is American in origin, although many stations use such Canadian services as Broadcast News as well. This trend will likely accelerate because it provides a means of acquiring high-quality programming at affordable prices.

Generally, since the rise of television, radio has been transformed from a national and mass medium to a local and specialized one. It continues to play an important role: consumers depend on their AM radios for timely and frequent information about local news, weather and driving conditions and on FM for music for most tastes. Advertisers still find radio a useful and flexible means of reaching local customers. These functions seem to be essential enough that they will not likely be soon usurped.

Movies

The "golden age of Canadian cinema," approximately the years 1946 to 1954, ended abruptly with the arrival of television. The decline in movie-going in the 1950s was also exacerbated by other social changes such as higher rates of automobile ownership and more frequent vacations.[9] Both television and movies are visual media offering primarily dramatic entertainment. Television's great advantage, of course, is that it is more convenient and free, once the initial investment is made in the set. By 1975 paid movie admissions dropped from a high of 263 million to 97 million. In a period when the population of Canada grew by 57 per cent, the number of visits to the movie theatre fell by 63 per cent.

The movie industry adapted in several ways. In the late 1950s the Hollywood studios became involved in producing both television shows and made-for-TV movies. The American TV and movie industries have since that time been inseparable. Because Canada lacked an independent production industry when television was introduced, Canadian TV stations either bought from the U.S. or produced their own programs in-house, although the trend today is strongly toward independent production on the American model.[10] Another consequence was a contraction of the movie distribution and exhibition systems. Theatres were closed, especially in smaller communities and suburbs; the number of movie screens in Canada fell from 3,554 to 1,488 between 1953 and 1975. Large theatres were chopped up into several smaller ones, and more specialized films were shown to more specialized audiences. Admission prices also rose rapidly. Movies catered increasingly to teenagers and young adults, and to audiences desiring more explicit sex and violence than television allowed.

In the early 1980s, after twenty years of relative stability, audience numbers abruptly dropped again, primarily as a result of the introduction of VCRs and pay-TV movie channels. Between 1981 and 1986 the number of movie screens fell a further 23 per cent and attendance 20 per cent. The average Canadian went to the movies only three times a year in the late 1980s. The popularity of moviegoing, especially for the 18-to-24 year old demographic group, has increased in the 1990s, however. In 1997-8 attendance hit a thirty-six year high of almost 98 million. The large theatre chains are rapidly building multiplex complexes which are full-scale entertainment centres. On the other hand, because of a proportionate decline in prices, movie-ticket purchases accounted for only 11 per cent of what Canadian families spent on entertainment in 1996, compared with 17 per cent in 1986. For many families, in-home entertainment (especially videos and cable TV) now grabs a larger portion of the entertainment budget.

Although the movies Canadians are flocking to see are almost entirely American (Canadian films get only 5 per cent of screen time), the Canadian film production industry has made some important gains. The creation of the Canadian Film Development Corporation in 1968 (renamed Telefilm Canada in 1983), along with tax incentives to encourage investment in Canadian films, stimulated production in the 1970s, although it did not solve the perennial problem of how to get the films distributed once they were made. In

1983, 14.6 per cent of the 474 films distributed in Canada were of Canadian origin, 18.6 per cent French and 54 per cent from the United States. The tax policy instituted in the 1970s encouraged a number of international co-productions that had some commercial success. In 1975 there were thirty-six feature films produced in Canada, thirty-four of them in the private sector. This compares with a total of *two* back in 1954. These numbers alone did not, however, particularly cheer the nationalists who thought that a Canadian film policy should be directed to encouraging films that explored and expressed the Canadian identity rather than simply to providing jobs in the industry and tax write-offs for the wealthy. In the 1980s and 1990s Telefilm aid encouraged the production of a number of culturally (and even occasionally commercially) successful Canadian films. The improvement is summed up in the following statistics: from 1913, when Canada's first feature film, "Evangeline," was produced, until 1967, 237 feature films were made in Canada; from 1968 to 1999, Telefilm alone supported the creation of 700 feature films.[11]

The film-distribution sector, however, remains externally dominated. The most popular and profitable films are still distributed by the subsidiaries of the American companies which own their American rights, and a new film act intended to give Canadian distributors more access to independently made foreign films was first watered down, then failed to pass through the Senate prior to the 1988 election, and has never been reintroduced. Two major exhibition chains dominate, Famous Players, owned by Viacom, and Cineplex-Odeon, owned by Loews. A third American chain, AMC, is also rapidly expanding in the Canadian exhibition market.

Like radio, movies essentially ceased to be a mass medium after the advent of television, but they did not die nor are they likely to do so. New markets on television and for rental videos will encourage continued movie production, and some customers will always prefer the social experience and larger screen of the commercial theatre. The Canadian film-production industry, as always, however, needs improved access to both commercial screens and television schedules in order to come in from the cultural periphery.

Magazines

The Canadian mass magazine industry was never strong. From the beginning, popular American periodicals of general interest outsold Canadian. Many of the American magazines sold in the Canadian market are what is called "overflow" circulation — that is, they are additional copies identical to those sold in the United States. Others differ only in that some of the advertising material is oriented to Canadian consumers, similar to split-run and regional editions of-fered to specialized advertisers within the United States. During and after the short lived tariff of the 1930s, a few American publishers also set up branch-plant Canadian editions of their magazines, con-taining some Canadian editorial material but relying for the most part on the parent company for copy. The most important of these in the modern era have been the Canadian editions of *Time* and *Reader's Digest* (and a French-language version, *Sélection du Reader's Digest*), both founded in the early 1940s.

Mass consumer magazines depend primarily on advertising for their income. In the 1950s the Canadian magazine industry's reve-nues were sharply reduced by competition from three sources: tele-vision, weekend supplements to the daily newspapers such as the *Star Weekly* and *Weekend*, and the rising popularity of *Time* and *Reader's Digest*. Amidst mounting cries from Canadian publishers for help, and reluctant or unable to interfere in the marketplace with respect to the first two competitors, in 1956 the Liberal government introduced a 20 per cent excise tax on advertising material in all "special editions" of American magazines. This action was justified by some rather compelling figures: while American magazines (in-cluding Canadian editions) had 67 per cent of the Canadian market in 1948, by 1954 this had risen to 80 per cent, and whereas *Time* and *Reader's Digest* had 18 per cent of the total ad revenues of the major general-interest magazines in 1948, in 1955 they had 37 per cent.[12] There were also rumours in the mid 1950s that a number of other American publications, possibly including *Newsweek*, were about to launch Canadian editions.

The tax was widely criticized, and in 1958, soon after the Conser-vatives came into office, they removed it. Five more American maga-zines promptly introduced Canadian editions, and several more began enticing Canadian advertisers with split runs. The ensuing controversy led the Diefenbaker government in 1960 to set up the Royal Commission on Publications, headed by Grattan O'Leary, editor of the Ottawa *Journal*. While the commissioners were asked to inquire into all aspects of the magazine industry, the terms of reference made it clear that the question of competition from Ameri-can magazines was to be the focus. The premises were also explicitly those of cultural nationalism: "Canadian magazines and periodicals add to the richness and variety of Canadian life and are essential to the culture and unity of Canada," stated the order-in-council setting up the commission.[13]

The O'Leary Commission concluded that overflow circulation of American magazines into Canada was unavoidable, but that something should be done about the unfair competition of split runs and regional and Canadian editions. The commissioners argued that a very considerable proportion of the editorial material in the Canadian editions of *Time* and *Reader's Digest* was identical to that in the American editions and available at much less than its true cost. This meant that these Canadian editions were very appealing to consumers and very profitable, that they were able to keep their advertising rates low, and that they therefore attracted Canadian advertisers who by rights should be supporting the domestic magazine industry.

The commissioners made two main recommendations aimed at encouraging Canadian advertisers to utilize Canadian magazines in preference to others: the tax deduction for expenses incurred in advertising should not be allowed for foreign periodicals; and foreign periodicals containing advertising explicitly aimed at Canadians should be excluded from entry under the Customs Act (this provision was to deal with split runs printed in the United States).

O'Leary and his colleagues insisted that their recommendations in no way involved a restriction on freedom of expression. Any magazine from anywhere in the world was welcome in Canada as long as it did not act as a vehicle for Canadian advertisements. In other words, the policy was positive — to divert Canadian advertising to its proper Canadian uses — not exclusionary.

The commissioners found that the problems of French-language consumer magazines were different from those of English. While overflow circulation of magazines from France had a considerable share of the newsstand market in Quebec, Canadian advertisers were not utilizing this medium, so competition for ad revenues was not a factor. The principal problem was that combined — and very attractive — rates were offered to advertisers who chose to use both *Reader's Digest* and *Sélection du Reader's Digest*, or Maclean-Hunter's combinations of *Chatelaine-La Revue Moderne* or *Maclean's-Le Magazine Maclean*. These deals did entice ad dollars from Quebec-owned journals, so the commissioners recommended that they no longer be allowed.

Before the Conservative government could act on the O'Leary recommendations it was defeated; not until 1965 was magazine legislation finally introduced, by the Liberals. While it enacted the essence of the two main O'Leary proposals, the Liberal government made a very important exception: foreign magazines that had been edited, printed and published in Canada in the twelve months ending April 26, 1965 were deemed Canadian for the purpose of the new rules. In other words, *Time* and *Reader's Digest* were exempted from the provisions. It was rumoured then and later — and denied by Prime Minister Lester Pearson — that this action was taken out of fear that American retaliation would jeopardize several Canada-U.S. trade deals then under negotiation, the most important of which was the Auto Pact.[14]

Over the next few years, the market dominance of the two Canadian editions continued to grow, and the situation of Canadian mass magazines became more desperate as the competition from television accelerated. The magazine industry in general saw its share of total advertising revenue fall from 4.2 per cent to 2.4 per cent, and by 1969 *Time* and *Reader's Digest* were taking 56 per cent of those revenues.[15] In 1966 these two publications, in cooperation with such Canadian magazines as *Maclean's*, *Chatelaine*, *Saturday Night* and *L'Actualité*, set up a magazine advertising bureau to coordinate and streamline their dealings with ad agencies. From this time on, criticism from these Canadian publishers of the special position of *Time* and *Reader's Digest* was muted, for they gained spill-over benefits from the attractiveness of the two Canadian editions to advertisers.

In 1969 Senator Keith Davey persuaded the Senate to set up a special committee to investigate the state of the mass media in Canada, particularly their influence and ownership. With respect to magazines, the Davey committee's members declared that "Magazines are special. Magazines constitute the only national press we possess in Canada." They went on:

> We believe that creeping continentalism has proceeded far enough in this country. We believe the present situation of the magazine industry is a perfect example of the dangers of an unexamined acceptance of foreign investment.... We deeply regret that *Time* and *Reader's Digest* were exempted from the O'Leary legislation. It was a bad decision.[16]

The Davey committee's report gave a boost to those unhappy with the 1965 law. In a climate of considerable pressure from cultural nationalists on a number of fronts, the Liberal government in early

1975 introduced Bill C-58, which finally fulfilled the O'Leary recommendations and eliminated the tax concessions enjoyed by *Time* and *Reader's Digest*.[17] (The bill, passed in February 1976, also disallowed the tax deductibility of ads on American border television stations.) *Time* ceased publishing its Canadian edition a few weeks later. The magazine is now available in Canada only in its American form, but because it still prints several regional editions in Canada, with very low advertising rates, it is still well used by Canadian advertisers. *Time* had a circulation of about 320,000 a week in Canada in 1999. *Reader's Digest* rearranged its affairs to qualify as Canadian under the legislation (although real control still lies in the United States) and so continues to be eligible for tax deductibility and to publish its Canadian editions. In 1999 the English edition had a circulation of slightly over 1 million in Canada.

The controversy leading up to Bill C-58 reveals much about the complicated interconnections between culture and economics in the Canadian mass media. On the one hand, Canadian advertisers indicated by their actions that they found the Canadian editions of *Time* and *Reader's Digest* to be effective instruments for the sale of their goods. Similarly, very large numbers of Canadians showed by their purchases that they appreciated the editorial material offered by the two magazines, whether it was Canadian or not. Editorial, printing and distribution jobs for Canadians were also created by the publication of these editions. Restricting the magazines thus hurt some Canadians. Many also construed government action in this area as interference with the freedom of the press.

On the other side was the viewpoint expressed by both official bodies that inquired into the subject: because the Canadian magazine industry was of vital national importance it must be saved by measures that augmented its income without meddling with either private ownership or editorial content. Given that advertising constituted the industry's principal source of revenue, attention to that factor seemed mandatory. While it might be admitted that competition from television and weekend supplements was at least as much the cause of the plight of Canadian periodicals as were *Time* and *Reader's Digest*, it was far more difficult both practically and politically to intervene in those areas. Bill C-58 could be justified as simply the removal of a privilege, not a fundamental interference with rights. *Time* and *Reader's Digest* retained their freedom to publish as Canadian editions — it was just made less profitable for them to do so.

on-line now — although exactly how they will recoup the money from lost sales is not clear.[20]

The big story of the last thirty years has been newspaper concentration. The decline of competition in the newspaper industry actually began around the First World War. In 1911 there were 143 daily newspapers published in Canada; there have never been as many since. At first in towns, then in small cities, then even in larger cities, closures created "one-paper towns." When the Davey committee made its report in 1970, it found that genuine newspaper competition existed in only five Canadian cities. By the time the Royal Commission on Newspapers looked at the industry in 1980–81, it concluded that "newspaper competition...is virtually dead in Canada."[21] This picture has changed somewhat since then. While many middle-sized cities now have only one daily paper, and others like Montreal do not have true competition because the four newspapers serve very different markets, in Toronto real competition, in format, ideology and presentation, has revived, especially with the arrival of the *National Post* in 1999. The story of that competition is much covered by the media, tending to divert attention from the monopoly situation in most Canadian cities.

At the same time as the number of dailies fell, their ownership has become more concentrated. Already by 1938 the Sifton and Southam interests between them owned almost 20 per cent of Canada's daily newspaper circulation. In 1960 the four largest owners controlled 36 per cent of circulation; by 1980 that figure had reached 65 per cent.

In late 1979 Thomson Newspapers, already owners of about thirty small papers scattered across Canada, purchased the eight dailies belonging to FP Publications, including the Toronto *Globe and Mail* and the Winnipeg *Free Press*, for $165 million. On August 27, 1980, Thomson shut down one of its acquisitions, the Ottawa *Journal*, and simultaneously Southam closed the Winnipeg *Tribune*. The result left Thomson's *Free Press* and Southam's *Citizen* the only dailies in Winnipeg and Ottawa respectively. On the same day Thomson sold its interests in the Montreal *Gazette* and Pacific Press (publisher of the Vancouver *Sun* and *Province*) to Southam. In one day ("Black Wednesday") four major cities lost English-language newspaper competition.[22] In the hue and cry that followed, the federal government laid conspiracy charges against the two firms under the Combines Investigation Act, but they were acquitted in 1983. Prime Minister Pierre Trudeau also quickly appointed a royal commission on newspapers, headed by Tom Kent, to study the industry and to recommend legal and policy changes.

The Kent commission analyzed all the logical economic causes that had led to such a high degree of monopoly and concentration in the Canadian newspaper industry and concluded that we had just drifted into a situation "clearly and directly contrary to the public interest." In its critique it distinguished, however, between chain and conglomerate ownership. The principal problem, according to the commissioners, was not so much that freedom of expression would be better served if newspapers were in more hands (although they did believe that), but that too many newspapers were owned by large conglomerates with interests in many areas other than publishing. (The Thomson and Irving organizations and Torstar Corporation were particularly noted.) Most alarming to the commissioners was the cynicism with which Canadians apparently regarded their newspaper press; a survey had found that only 29 per cent of Canadians felt newspapers were the most fair and unbiased news source (TV got 53 per cent) and only 23 per cent felt they were the most influential (TV got 67 per cent). Because readers knew that corporate owners set the tone, the parameters and the budget for their operations, the commissioners concluded, newspapers had lost their credibility and legitimacy. Even the appearance of conflict of interest is fatal, they argued, to the ideal of a free press.

The commissioners, therefore, made a series of recommendations concerning divestment, bans on expanded cross-ownership with other local media, tax incentives to encourage expenditure on editorial content and the creation of a press rights panel. In response to one of these points, in 1982 the government instructed the CRTC to deny new broadcasting licences or renewals to applicants who owned a daily newspaper in the same market. The directive allowed for exceptions "in the public interest" however, which turned out (before the policy was withdrawn by the Mulroney government) to mean most cases. In 1986, a new competition act was also passed, which may possibly inhibit future mergers. Its first test in the area of publishing, however, concerning the purchase of two Vancouver-area newspapers by Southam, which already controlled both Vancouver dailies, resulted in a ruling that was largely a victory for Southam. None of the other recommendations of the Kent commission has ever been enacted.

Today the Canadian newspaper industry is considerably more concentrated than the levels that so alarmed the Kent commissioners.

In 1996 Conrad Black's Hollinger took control of the Southam chain, after having already absorbed the Sifton papers. Hollinger now owns 60 of Canada's 105 dailies. Thomson's holdings have been whittled down to 9 dailies, and most of those are for sale as this is being written. Sun Media owns 15 dailies, and Quebecor, Power Corporation and the Irving family another 4 each. Large corporations with diverse international interests and no local roots now own 93 per cent of national circulation.

The Kent commission addressed a question that goes far beyond newspapers. In all the media, concentration and conglomerate ownership is increasingly the norm. A few large corporations whose names could be listed on the fingers of both hands control a very high proportion of our mass communication outlets. This situation, certainly not unique to Canada, is the result of "natural" economic forces that favour reducing competition to decrease risk and raise profits, and of societal and governmental reluctance to interfere with the free marketplace or "freedom of the press." But as the Kent commissioners pointed out in 1981, what freedom of the press really means in such circumstances is "only that enormous influence without responsibility is conferred on a handful of people."[23] Whether the tendency to concentration and chain ownership has a measurable effect on newspaper content specifically, remains a matter for debate. The Kent commission's analysis rested more on assertion than proof; subsequent studies have drawn mixed conclusions.[24] Further empirical studies clearly are desirable.

Since the 1950s, the technological and economic imperatives of the mass media have led us to a situation where the voices are few and the tunes they sing similar — and often American. Whether the next wave of technological innovation will reverse this trend or exacerbate it remains to be seen. If we, or our government, are to exert any control over the process, we must understand the complex of economic, cultural and technological factors which constitute our mass media today.

4

The Economics of
the Mass Media

All communications systems have economic ramifications. This is especially the case for the mass media, because of their central role in modern capitalist economies. We often refer to the mass media by the rather anomalous term cultural (or content) industries. The expression implies that, while the product is a cultural form (art, entertainment, opinion or information), it is being manufactured and distributed in the same manner as such consumer goods as detergents or jeans — by privately owned corporate enterprises utilizing mass-production methods, advanced technology and sophisticated distribution systems to reach the largest possible number of customers. More precisely, cultural goods created by individuals or groups are carried to audiences by means of mass-manufactured instruments. This juxtaposition of cultural and economic functions lies at the root of many of the difficulties in coming to terms with the role of the mass media in our society.

The situation is further complicated by one significant difference between the mass media and most other consumer goods. In the ordinary marketplace, to put it at its simplest, the producer makes the good and the consumer buys it. But with the exception of films, the mass media being discussed here are not primarily financed by direct consumer purchase. Instead they are offered partially or totally "free" to their audiences, the cost being picked up by advertisers who are thereby given access to potential buyers for their products and who in turn pass the cost on in the prices they charge. In one sense, then, the advertisers are the real purchasers of the cultural goods; they choose to buy those they believe (or have evidence to prove) will bring with them the most, and the most contented, consumers. In a very real way, what the advertisers are purchasing is not the cultural product but the audience.[1]

As even the briefest of comparisons with other countries reveals, it is not inevitable that the media should be supported in this way. There are alternative methods of ownership and financing possible — individual subscribers, voluntary organizations, churches, states. Some of these other methods are even used occasionally in North America. For the various historical reasons outlined in the first three chapters, however, private ownership and advertiser financing have become predominant in the mass media on this continent, and that is unlikely to change.

One of the most important of these reasons has been the rise of the consumer-goods manufacturing sector. The mass media are the principal instruments by which demand for consumer goods is created. Manufacturers need the mass media to convince the individuals who collectively form the mass market to buy their mass-produced goods. The economic viability of the media is thus always a matter of considerable concern to North American manufacturers and other advertisers. In other, less consumption-oriented societies, the media serve other goals and thus are funded in other ways. All of these economic realities, of course, have cultural repercussions.

Private Enterprise

The fundamental economic fact about our mass media industries is that with a couple of partial exceptions they are made up of private enterprises owned by corporations and individuals for the purpose of making a profit. Like other businessmen, media owners desire to minimize their costs and maximize their prices. They also strive to control and expand their markets and to decrease risks. With the profits accrued, they invest in other enterprises, often also in the communications field. All of these "natural" processes have consequences. If media entrepreneurs are not able to make a satisfactory profit, they go out of business. Then the cultural vehicles do not exist at all. As the late Quebec publisher Pierre Péladeau put it: "The name of the game is profit. If you don't make a profit, you don't have a newspaper."[2]

But what is a satisfactory profit, and how can it be measured against the cultural role of the media? Most studies have indicated that the cultural industries are at least as profitable as other industrial sectors in Canada. Everyone is familiar with Lord Thomson's famous aphorism that owning a television station is like having a licence to print money. Strict comparisons are difficult to make because calculations are frequently based on different criteria and are subject to much interpretation. It seems, however, that after a roller-coaster decade, by the end of the 1990s profitability had been restored to the Canadian television and cable industries, that private radio was back on a very good financial footing, that the periodical industry was holding its own, and that newspaper profits were at a 25-year high. What continues to concern cultural analysts is that the drive to maintain levels of profitability and to perform well on stock markets has led media corporations to cost-minimizing tactics that have resulted in cultural products that are, by some criteria at least, inferior, and to a concentration of ownership that has decreased the diversity of points of view available to our society. Out of economic forces have come cultural problems.

Minimizing Costs

The "editorial" content of a newspaper, a magazine, or a radio or television show — that is, the articles and the programs — costs the publisher or broadcaster money. It is not the only expense involved in bringing the product to the consumer; there are also material costs (like newsprint), distribution costs (like transmitters) and administrative costs, among others. For maximum profit, all must be kept as low as possible without losing readers or viewers. But the struggle to minimize editorial costs has the most obvious cultural impact.

Quite simply, this economic incentive drives many Canadian media owners to purchase cheap editorial material from abroad (mainly the United States) rather than to produce it themselves. Because of the size of the American domestic market and the fact that it is by taste and custom virtually closed to foreign media wares, American manufacturers of popular cultural products are able to lavish large amounts of money on their goods and yet still make a profit. The average cost of an episode of an American television serial in 1998 was $1.5 million; "ER" cost NBC a whopping $13 million per episode. The writers and stars on such shows are paid enormous salaries, and large sums are spent on the technical side to make the show look slick and professional ("high production values"). These costs can, however, be recovered on first- and second-run sales in the large American market; after that, any money the program can make in foreign sales is profit. Thus for a very reasonable price the American producer is happy to sell the rights to the program to a Canadian television station or network. The Canadian broadcaster is then able to offer his advertisers and viewers the "best" of American television at bargain-basement prices. Richard Collins in the early 1990s cited the example of "St. Elsewhere," which cost about $750,000 an hour to produce, but was available to Canadian broadcasters simultaneously with American for $30,000.[3]

Obviously, profits accrue to the broadcaster when a popular program can be purchased for much less than it cost to make, and when advertisers flock to buy commercial time on it. But the private broadcaster's disincentive to purchase or produce Canadian programs is even greater because often domestic shows not only do not generate profits, they actually cause losses. CTV estimated in 1990–1 that its "typical" Canadian entertainment program cost $112,500 per hour to produce but brought in revenues of only $69,600 — for a loss of $43,000. Meanwhile, a typical American show cost $60,000 (to buy) but yielded revenues of $116,000 — a profit of $56,000. Therefore the "opportunity cost" — what it actually cost the network to use Canadian rather than American shows — was $99,000 per hour.[4] Clearly, all the economic incentives lie in the direction of spending as little as possible on Canadian content; often when Canadian shows are produced, budgets are kept low, so audience appeal is weak and ad revenues mediocre — in other words, they become self-fulfilling prophecies.

The results have been and still are demonstrable on our television screens nightly. In 1984–5, 86 per cent of the money spent by Canadian television broadcasters on the purchase of foreign programming was spent by the private broadcasters. For $133 million, English-language private broadcasters bought shows that probably cost at least $3 billion to produce. As the Caplan-Sauvageau Task Force remarked, "It is not surprising that private broadcasters find this an attractive proposition, particularly when these shows come with the backing of extensive publicity and advertising that spills into the Canadian market."[5] While the cost of American shows has risen recently owing to increased production costs and more competitive markets, imported programs are still a bargain for Canadian broadcasters.[6] The structure of the main private network, CTV, which until the late 1990s was a cooperative of member stations each intent on maximizing its own profits, also encouraged the tendency to purchase abroad. The arrival of CanWest Global as the third national network has not improved the situation: until recently its expenditure on Canadian content was as much as 50 per cent *less* than CTV's. In both cases, the networks allocate to Canadian production only the minimum necessary to abide by CRTC rulings; it would not be good business to do otherwise.[7]

The example of television, while the best known, is not unique, although in the print media the process of reducing editorial costs by importing foreign material works somewhat differently. Because of their nature, daily newspapers rely quite heavily on internally produced editorial material. Approximately two-thirds of the average daily is written by its own staff. Again, however, the owner faces an incentive to reduce that cost as much as possible. One way of doing so (and much easier in these days of one-paper cities) is to cut staff to the bone, reduce local coverage, hire young reporters or freelancers at minimal wages, and so on. Up to a certain point, readership will not fall with the quality because there are few alternatives. Veteran Canadian journalist and professor Peter Desbarats described the effect of bottom-line thinking on newspaper content succinctly:

> When journalists come to understand that the bottom line is more important than editorial excellence, that media owners regard editorial costs as, at best, a necessary evil ... they perform accordingly. Editors begin to give preference to journalists who are good at the "quick and dirty," who can produce a flow of usable if not notable material. Journalists either adapt to this or leave for jobs in other fields ... Eventually a tradition of quick, shoddy journalism develops, with value placed on negative stories that can shock and attract attention. This process is now well advanced in some Canadian newsrooms.[8]

Newspapers that spend more than strictly necessary on editorial costs, that is, that sacrifice some profits to public service, become targets for takeover. Because of their lower profitability, they can be purchased relatively cheaply, and then by strict cost-cutting turned into real money-makers. A number of authorities in the 1980s suggested that Southam Inc., English-Canada's dominant chain, was particularly vulnerable in this respect. Southam's attempts to save itself through a contentious share swap with Torstar Corporation, extensive layoffs, administrative centralization and other measures were in vain; Conrad Black's Hollinger Inc. took control of Southam in the mid-1990s. Within eighteen months, Southam's profits had quadrupled, largely due to what journalism professor John Miller terms "the scythe ... that swept through its workforce."[9]

In addition to saving money by using cheaper internally produced material, newspapers can reduce expenditures by sharing editorial costs with others. Newspapers in several cities owned by one corporation, for example, can hire a single columnist to cover the Ottawa scene or the financial markets, an expense no one of them could bear alone without severely cutting into profits. The cooperative news agency owned by Canadian newspaper publishers, Canadian Press, offers somewhat similar economies. Not only do the member papers exchange local news with one another, thus providing everyone with plenty of copy, but CP itself has correspondents in Ottawa and a few foreign capitals whose reports are available to all.

Again, as in the case of television, Canadian newspapers can save even more money if they import editorial material from the United States. Syndicated American columnists and comics fill up many pages in our daily newspapers. Canadian Press also economizes by buying almost all its foreign news from Associated Press and then re-writing it for Canadian consumption. Paying two or three staff writers in New York costs far less than supporting numerous foreign correspondents around the world.

The private radio industry provides another instance of the same economic reality. At least 50 per cent of the air time on AM radio stations consists of recordings, and an even higher percentage on FM stations. The majority of the records played are American in origin, the products of a large, dynamic and highly competitive sound-recording industry in the United States. Canadian radio broadcasters save money by using this cheap and varied, mainly foreign, programming. The Canadian recording industry, in comparison, is small and struggling, although it produces the majority of records made by Canadian artists.[10] Private radio stations would find it very expensive indeed to produce enough programming to fill up all their hours on the air without access to American records.

Magazines are another case again. Very little of the editorial material in Canadian magazines is imported, which is one reason the industry has struggled for profitability compared to some of the other media. Prior to 1976, as already explained in Chapter 3, the Canadian editions of *Time* and *Reader's Digest* did act as vehicles for the import of much cheap foreign editorial material. Bill C-58, the amendment to the Income Tax Act that made it disadvantageous for Canadian advertisers to use the two Canadian editions, was passed precisely because they were viewed as a serious threat to the revenues of the rest of the Canadian magazine industry with its higher editorial costs. Nevertheless, sufficient loopholes were left in the legislation that it remains possible for two magazines that technically satisfy the Canadian ownership requirements of Bill C-58, namely

Reader's Digest and *TV Guide*, to continue to contain a significant amount of imported American content, and to flourish. In the late 1990s *Sports Illustrated* used a technological loophole to begin publishing a split-run edition for the Canadian market, full of Canadian advertising but little Canadian editorial content. Despite various manoeuvres by the Canadian government, the World Trade Organization (WTO) ruled that Canada must allow such split-runs. Pessimists in the magazine industry speculate that as much as half of Canadian advertising revenues will be lost to Canadian magazines and that many of the smaller ones will go under, despite the government's promise to attempt to shore them up with direct subsidies.

In general, then, the desire to keep costs down has tended to lead private Canadian media owners to spend as little as possible on editorial material. The cultural content of the media is viewed by many owners as a cost to be minimized. In most instances that has meant importing considerable quantities of less expensive and less risky foreign-originated material. Despite legislation preventing or discouraging foreign ownership of Canadian media enterprises, foreign content prevails.

Concentration

Another way private media owners maximize profits is by gaining monopolistic or oligopolistic control of the marketplace. In recent years, Canadian cultural industries have been characterized by increasing concentration, the coalescence of production or distribution or both into fewer and fewer and larger and larger hands. This has taken a number of different forms, especially chain ownership, cross-ownership and vertical integration. Media industries were also heavily implicated in the corporate takeover spree of the 1980s and 1990s, which left many of them both more concentrated and more indebted. A few figures graphically illustrate how pervasive oligopolistic concentration is in the cultural industries today (as, indeed, in many other areas of the economy). According to the latest available figures, 70 per cent of Canada's daily newspapers are in the hands of two publishers (60 per cent of circulation); 58 per cent of television stations are owned by five broadcasters; two-thirds of cable TV subscriptions are controlled by three companies; 50 per cent of movie theatres and 60 per cent of screens are owned by the two largest chains; and four major publishers share at least 90 per cent of the total ad revenues earned by Canadian consumer magazines.

One of the major causes of concentration is the economic principle of economies of scale. A good example of this principle is "first copy cost," which can be demonstrated simply with the example of a newspaper. Many of the expenses involved in producing a daily paper are incurred before a single sheet is run off the press; the costs of reporters, buildings, presses and press workers, wire service, editors and so on must all be carried no matter how many copies are printed in the end. Obviously, then, it is economically preferable to spread these fixed costs out over as large a readership as possible. While some lesser expenses like those for newsprint and trucking will rise with increasing sales, the first copy cost per person falls. It is more advantageous therefore to produce on a large scale. Newspapers also gain economies of scale in terms of the number of pages they publish; a forty-eight-page paper is cheaper to publish per page than one of thirty-six pages. In another case, it is the distribution that becomes less expensive per unit with expanding audience. For example, it costs no more to distribute a television show from a transmitting tower to one million customers within range than to ten. Obviously, it is more efficient to have the million.

In all these instances, a comparative advantage accrues to the outlet with the bigger audience. The economic consequences are straightforward: a larger newspaper, magazine or TV station will in all probability eventually drive a smaller one out of business. The result is concentration — more of the media in the hands of fewer owners. This may be seen as a perfectly "natural" process caused by the search for efficiency in the marketplace.

The fact that most media are primarily financed by advertising revenue reinforces the process. Larger units are able to offer advertisers better rates; the advertisers find it not only cheaper but easier to deal with only one outlet. One newspaper advertising manager described how this process helped destroy the Winnipeg *Tribune* and give the *Free Press* a monopoly in that city:

> The turning point for the *Tribune* came, I believe, in the late 1950s when Simpsons-Sears opened their first store at the new Polo Park Shopping Centre. We were quite pleased that a new advertiser had appeared on the market, but our joy was short-lived. We were very soon to learn that the policy of this U.S.-influenced management company was such that they demanded domination of the media with the largest circulation, and they chose to interpret "media" as a choice between two newspapers

.... They paid no heed to the long-time practice of Eaton's and the Bay, who placed virtually equal linage in both papers so as to reach the total market.[11]

While concentration at the production and distribution stage in a cultural industry may occur "naturally" as the result of economies of scale, as American media economist Bruce M. Owen points out, concentration often occurs at other stages in the cultural production process as well, as a result of the practice of vertical integration.[12] Take the example of a newspaper again. While the heavy capital investment involved in purchasing press equipment may lead eventually to the existence of only one press in each city, it is not necessarily inevitable that this press produce only one newspaper. Yet for the most part this is what occurs. Why? Because those who own the presses need to be sure there will be something to print on them each day; to be certain of supply, they prefer to employ the writers and editors as well. Newspapers own their own distribution systems for the same reason.

The classic case of vertical integration occurred in the movie industry in the United States in the 1920s. In that instance those who controlled the editing stage, the major studios, also took control of creation, distribution and exhibition in order to decrease the risks to their costly investments. The result was disastrous for independent Canadian film producers. Various attempts by the Canadian government to encourage private Canadian film production have floundered on the reality that it is very difficult for the films, once made, to get theatrical distribution. Most of the largest film distributors in Canada are American-based, and many are under joint ownership with production companies. They distribute almost no Canadian films; it is easier for them to concentrate their attention on the same American product they handle in the United States. The many small Canadian distributors, who handle 95 per cent of the Canadian films produced, have only 14 per cent of the theatrical market.

Distributors also reinvest their profits in the production of more films. American distributors are less likely to invest in Canadian films; a large portion of their profits flow out of the country to finance more Hollywood production. Exhibitors, in turn, claim that there is little demand for Canadian films; here economies of scale in marketing and publicity are the significant factor. Canadians are deluged with spillover from the average $24 million that major Hollywood studios spend advertising each of their films; Canadian films average $3 million *for total production costs.* The result of all these factors is that Canadian films are squeezed into the cracks in the American-dominated booking schedules; they fill only 3 or 4 per cent of total screen time in Canadian movie theatres.

There are, however, some recent signs of improvement in the Canadian feature-film sector. A few entrepreneurial Canadian producers are aggressively taking advantage of opportunities opening up for foreign sales (through co-productions) and in the video and specialty television markets. While the same distributors control the latter markets, their size and diversity permit better access for Canadian distributors and for independently produced films, and in fact Canada has now become the world's second largest exporter of audiovisual products.

Like the movie industry, the magazine industry feels significant effects from concentration at the distribution stage. Magazines are sold both by subscription (delivered through the postal system) and on newsstands. On average, Canadian magazines have a ratio of about 80/20 subscription to newsstand sales, while foreign (American) magazines sold in Canada are at almost the opposite ratio, 30/70. The difference is significant, because although subscriptions provide a guaranteed circulation, they are very expensive to attract and retain; newsstand sales are becoming an increasingly important part of the magazine market and are more profitable. One of the major reasons for the domination of American magazines on newsstands is the distribution system. Almost all the national magazine distributors are American-controlled, most of them owned by American publishing firms. These distributors supply a number of regional wholesalers, largely Canadian-owned, who in turn deal with retail outlets. All levels of the chain are dependent on the national distributors, and are influenced by their choice of product. Not surprisingly, magazine distributors, like their film counterparts, prefer to deal in large quantities of the same American magazines that they handle in their home market, and they ensure that these products are given the most promotion and best display space. The result is less exposure for Canadian magazines, their greater dependence on less-profitable subscription sales, and financial difficulties, especially for the smaller magazines.

Chain ownership, or horizontal integration, is another version of concentration. Here economies are gained by centralizing certain functions. The example of hiring a single columnist for an entire newspaper chain has already been mentioned. Advertising departments and managerial skills can also be somewhat consolidated under chain ownership. The Thomson organization was particularly renowned for saving money by the application of sophisticated managerial techniques to all its papers. (Some former Thomson employees swear that they were required to relinquish the stub of their old pencil before they could have a new one!) More important, because a chain is a much larger corporate entity, it can raise the capital necessary for technological development more easily. It can also use its collective strength to survive a circulation war in a single city to drive out an independent. This is one of the main reasons the vast majority of Canadian cities have only one daily.

It should not be concluded, however, that no competition exists in the newspaper world. What is called the "umbrella" effect applies in many cities with monopoly dailies. Readers have access not only to the local journal, but also to some extent to larger regional or national papers and to weekly community papers (a rapidly-growing sector). Additionally, of course, there is competition among media; radio and television provide alternative sources of information for residents of the one-paper town. Yet, there is some doubt whether this situation is a truly competitive one. Each medium serves a different purpose and has a different orientation, both in terms of content and of advertising. To that extent they are more complementary than competitive.

Of even greater significance is the very extensive cross-ownership of the media in Canada today. Most of the major corporations in the cultural sector have holdings in several media, sometimes in the same community. A few examples give just a suggestion of how pervasive — and complex — cross-ownership and corporate convergence have become, and the extent to which these corporations have moved into new media, especially the Internet. While Rogers Communications, for example, still receives over 44 per cent of its revenues from its wireless telephone business, Rogers Cantel, 36 per cent comes from its cable company (controlling over 70 per cent of the subscriber base in Ontario), and 19 per cent from its media interests (radio stations, Internet sites, the portal Rogers@home, and most importantly the former Maclean-Hunter magazine empire which includes most of Canada's major consumer magazines such as *Macleans, Chatelaine,* and their French equivalents *L'Actualité* and *Châtelaine*). If Rogers succeeds in purchasing Vidéotron, Quebec's largest cable company, its reach will extend even further. Another large western cable company, Shaw Communications, also has interests in a number of specialty channels such as YTV, The Comedy Network, Teletoon and Country Music Television, and has almost complete dominance in the distribution of TV signals via satellite through its control of Cancom and StarChoice (in which Rogers also has a minority interest). Meanwhile, Bell Canada, whose traditional business has been in local and long distance telephone service and equipment, is now divesting itself of Nortel in favour of such ventures as an alliance with Sun Media to develop an Internet portal, and its parent company, BCE, owns ExpressVu direct-to-home satellite service and is on the verge of taking over the CTV network along with its specialty channels such as TSN, Newsnet and Discovery. Conrad Black's Hollinger, Inc., which owns or controls more than half of Canada's daily newspapers, is mainly a publishing company, with newspaper interests in Britain, the United States and Israel as well as Canada, but it has also begun divesting itself of many weekly newpapers in order to move more actively into Internet services such as Canada.com. Through its control of the Southam newspaper chain, and the creation of the *National Post* (incorporating the *Financial Post*), Hollinger holds the commanding position in the Canadian newspaper business; Sun Media, with 11 papers to Hollinger's 60, is a distant second. Usurped by Hollinger, the Thomson Corporation is leaving the Canadian newspaper business except for its flagship, the Toronto *Globe and Mail*; it now describes itself as an "information company," with worldwide interests in information services, book publishing, software, and advertising. In Quebec, one of the largest players is Quebecor, owner of Sun Media and extensive commercial printing operations in the United States. In early 2000 it sold its interest in forestry company Donohue Inc. in order to position itself for more involvement in broadcasting, cable and the Internet (it already owns Canoe, Canada's largest Internet portal). The other major Quebec player, Telemedia, has interests mainly in magazine publishing (for example *Canadian Living, TV Guide, Coup de Pouce* and *Madame au Foyer*) and radio broadcasting (76 stations across the country including Montreal's oldest station, CKAC-AM). In early 2000 it sold its magazine division to GTC Transcontinental in order to focus more on the broadcasting side of its business.

This type of concentration and cross-media ownership is not unique to Canada. A world-wide trend toward global corporations (a trend that seems to have reached a record-breaking pace in the early months of 2000) is as evident in the media/communications sector as in many others. The world's largest media company is Time

Warner, which controls not only magazine publisher Time Inc., but Warner Bros. (movies, TV programs and videos), Home Box Office, cable TV network CNN, WB Television Network, and the Atlanta Braves. In early 2000 Time Warner purchased British music company EMI; it already owned Warner Music Group and therefore now controls approximately 25 per cent of the world's music market. Around the same time Time Warner merged with AOL, a leading American Internet provider, creating a conglomerate of both old and new media so huge it is difficult to comprehend. The next-largest media company is also American, the Walt Disney Company, owners of ABC Television, Buena Vista Motion Pictures, Miramax, shares in nine specialty cable companies including ESPN, as well of course as its theme parks and movie studios. Other huge media corporations are also notable for the diversity of their holdings: Rupert Murdoch's News Corp., for example, owns most of Australia's newspapers and about one-third of those in Britain, including the prestigious *Times*, 20th Century Fox movie studios, the Fox TV network, the *New York Post*, HarperCollins publishing company and BSkyB satellite service in Britain. Murdoch is, according to *Time Magazine*, "the very model of the modern media mogul."[13] A partial listing of the holdings of Viacom (MTV and other specialty cable channels, Paramount Pictures, Blockbuster, Simon and Schuster publishers and — last but not least — the CBS television network) and Bertelsmann AG of Germany (Random House publishers, BMG Entertainment, a stake in barnesandnoble.com, many magazines) reveals the same international and multi-media diversification.

The business strategy of these companies is rooted in vertical integration: the entertainment industry's need for vast financial resources, the communications industry's need for "entertainment software," and the pressure on both groups to secure positions in electronic communications software, technology and commerce — all in the context of increasing globalization of markets.

Canadian media companies have been saved from foreign takeovers by domestic ownership laws, mainly the tax laws that discourage advertising in non-Canadian media. As the examples above indicate, however, several of the larger Canadian firms are active in foreign markets. This inconsistency has not gone unnoticed, particularly in protectionist circles in the United States. Similar and interrelated economic forces are driving the trend toward both national and international communications empires. On both levels, this extensive concentration of media power in the hands of a few has raised alarms.

Concentration, even cross-media ownership, is not necessarily a bad thing. It can be advantageous not only to the owner but often to others as well. A television station that belongs to a network can offer better programs because the cost of each is spread more widely. A newspaper that is a member of a chain might be able to survive in a competitive environment that would kill an independent. A concentrated Canadian industry can better defend itself against external takeovers. Too much competition can be as disastrous to quality as too little, resulting in nothing better than "wasteful imitation, redundancy and poorer quality in slicker packaging."[14] In other words, competition can be inefficient, and concentration can enable cross-subsidization of otherwise unprofitable ventures. Moreover, it can be argued that in this multi-media society consumers have many sources of information; a monopoly or oligopoly in one medium is counter-acted by the many other outlets available.

Thus, if we want to understand and deal with the issue of concentration in the media, we should remember that it results for the most part from economic forces operating naturally in a private enterprise economy and that it may even in some instances benefit consumers individually and society generally. Nevertheless, serious doubts have been raised about whether such "natural" outcomes as heavy import of foreign culture and highly concentrated corporate ownership are truly beneficial to Canadians. Before we turn to an examination of how economists have wrestled with that question, the role of advertising in our cultural industries needs special attention.

Advertising

Most of the money businesses spend on advertising goes to the mass media. Most of the financing of the mass media comes from advertising. The link is symbiotic.

Advertising agencies act as the intermediaries between the media and the advertisers. Ad agencies originated in the late nineteenth century when both mass-consumer industries and the mass media also began. Because of their earliest function as space-sellers for newspapers, ad agencies to this day remain the clients of the media, rather than of the advertisers. For a fee of approximately 15 per cent of the total cost, the ad agency takes responsibility for research, planning and booking of the advertisements, although recently the trend has been for this task to be taken over by specialized media-buying agencies. This leaves the ad agencies with the other part of their traditional job: the responsibility for producing the ad or commercial or hiring an independent production company to do so. This cost, which can run up to more than $150,000 for a thirty-second commercial, is then passed along to the advertiser.

The realities of the advertising market tend to favour larger firms. In order to maintain stability in their own businesses, media organizations place requirements of size and billing capacity on ad agencies before they will deal with them. Already by 1970 there was a tendency toward the merger of small Canadian firms into continental ones, a tendency that accelerated in the 1980s and 1990s to the point that most of the top advertising agencies in Canada are foreign owned. Many of the most heavily advertised consumer goods are produced by large American-based corporations with branch plants in Canada. Often they use the same ad agency — its head office in New York and its subsidiary in Canada. Sometimes they simply use the same ads in both countries, cutting into film-production and acting jobs in Canada. Even Canadian companies are having some of their ads produced in the United States, partly because the tariff on imported commercial film fell under the Free Trade Agreement. Soon Canada's major media outlets may derive most of their income from foreign-owned advertisers via foreign-owned ad agencies.

In 1998, about $10 billion was spent on advertising in the traditional media in Canada, up from about $6 billion in 1991. Media advertising is not only a huge business in Canada, but one upon which the cultural industries depend. Daily newspapers receive the greatest proportion of total ad expenditure, about 24.4 per cent in 1988, television 15.5 per cent, radio 8.5 per cent, and all periodicals 12.7 per cent. About 63 per cent of the revenue of consumer magazines comes from ads, 94 per cent of broadcasting revenues, and 80 per cent of newspapers'. In the United States, per-capita expenditure on advertising is about one-third more than in Canada, and it is distributed differently. Paul Audley points out that in general those Canadian media that depend primarily on local advertising, like radio and newspapers, earn ad revenues approximately equal (per-capita) to those in the United States. However, the Canadian media dependent on national advertising, like magazines and television, have per-capita revenues far lower than their American counterparts.

There are several reasons for this, including the fact that Americans read more magazines and watch more TV than Canadians do, but the most important cause is spillover advertising. About 70 per cent of the ads that Canadians read in American magazines are applicable in Canada. By this vehicle, American multinational companies have a free or at least a very inexpensive ride into the Canadian market, which reduces their incentive to spend money on ads in Canadian magazines, and therefore lessens the income of Canadian magazines.[15] The same holds true for advertisements on American television stations watched in Canada. About 80 per cent of the ads shown on the American networks are for products of multinational corporations available in both countries. This obviously reduces the incentive of American advertisers to buy time on Canadian stations because they know that much of the Canadian audience can receive the American networks.

In general, spillover advertising is much less a factor in newspapers or radio stations because of their local base. This, of course, is the crux of Audley's point. Local Canadian media do not face competition in either audience or advertising with external outlets, and so they attract their "fair" share of ad dollars. It is the national media, which must compete against spillover circulation and advertising, that are deprived of their natural revenue sources. The effect is clear: a reduction in the ability of these media to compete equally in their own market. Also, not incidentally, Canadian firms are thereby deprived of strong national media in which to advertise to their own customers nation-wide. Advertising is the financial mainstay of our mass media and, barring a radical structural transformation, will remain so. Thus these allocation problems are central to any strategies concerning stimulation of the national media.

Over the years, there has been much concern about the extent to which advertisers control media content. Tales abound about newspapers pulling stories critical of large department stores for fear of losing their business, or about television stations substituting light and happy fluff for heavy drama because the advertiser does not want the audience either thoughtful or gloomy. Some of the anecdotes are quite amusing. In the 1950s, apparently, American tobacco companies made sure that cigarettes were always smoked "gracefully" on the shows they sponsored, that the actors never coughed, that "disreputable" persons were never seen with cigarettes, and that fires never figured in the plot. More recently, and more seriously, a seven-year study of American magazines that accepted cigarette advertising showed that none of them ever printed a single article about the "medical and social havoc" wreaked by smoking. In a Canadian example, Air Canada apparently threatened to cancel newspaper ads if they appeared anywhere within two pages of stories about airline crashes or hijackings. A much-publicized case in the early 1990s concerned the boycott of the independent newspaper the *Kingston Whig-Standard* by local real-estate agencies because they did not like an article it published about how to sell your own home; the agencies switched their business to a Torstar-owned tabloid, *Kingston This Weekend*, and hurt the *Whig-Standard* enough that it was eventually sold to the Southam chain.[16]

While such actions no doubt do occur, the real influence of advertisers on the media is both more indirect and more structural. An advertiser very rarely has to withdraw or threaten to withdraw his ad; the newspaper editors and TV programmers *know* what is wanted, and self-censor, often almost unconsciously. From a wider perspective, this is because the ad business and the media business have grown up together and interdependently. They are both integral parts of our free-enterprise, consumption-oriented, affluent society. As the Davey report put it:

> Broadly speaking the advertisers, their agencies, and the media owners are all the same kind of people, doing the same kind of thing, within the same kind of private-enterprise rationale. There is nothing sinister about it, nothing conspiratorial. Advertiser pressure is not necessary because the influence is there anyway — subtly and by implication.[17]

What effect does advertising-financing really have on the content of the media? It is a truism that advertisers want access to the largest possible number of consumers, so they pay more to utilize the medium with the largest audience. Advertising rates are calculated according to the "cost per thousand" readers, listeners or viewers. This has tended to encourage the content with the widest possible appeal, or perhaps better, the content that offends the fewest. The lowest common denominator of taste is blessed with support; minorities are ignored.

This is a somewhat over-simplistic view, however. For one thing, not only advertising is to blame for bland and undistinguished content. Economists have demonstrated that the neglect of minority tastes occurs in any industry in which monopoly or monopolistic competition exists.[18] Additionally, advertisers are much more sophisticated than this explanation assumes. They want to target not simply the largest audience, but the one most likely to buy their particular product — as distinguished by age, sex, lifestyle and so on. This is most obvious in the case of magazines, where the vehicles are quite specialized and advertisers are very selective about which ones they utilize. It is increasingly true of newspaper and television markets as well with the birth of tabloids and specialty channels. It remains fundamental, however, that because of advertiser-driven economics, the media target those with money. No one is much interested in audiences of the poor.

The search for just the "right" program and "right" ad for the "right" audience has become a very sophisticated procedure. Market research began in the United States as early as 1911 and by the 1930s included sophisticated instruments like "audimeters" and Gallup polls. Today ad agencies and research organizations spend a great deal of time and money on audience research. No longer is it sufficient to know how many are watching a given TV show by having selected households fill in viewing diaries. Now individual television sets are connected through telephone lines and microprocessors to central computers monitoring the set every few seconds. In more sophisticated systems members of survey households punch in and out on a "people meter" as they enter and leave the TV room. In 1989, the A.C. Nielson Co., one of the two major Canadian audience-research firms, switched from diaries to people meters for its national surveys; the resulting (apparent) drop in network viewing totals shook both the television and advertising industries. Now people meters can also check for VCR usage, and both Nielson and BBM (the other main audience-research firm) are currently converting their systems to prepare to measure digital broadcasting.

Advertisers are becoming dissatisfied with simply knowing the demographics of audiences for particular programs, however. Now they also want to know how interested and involved the audience is, whether viewers enjoyed and valued the programs they watched or not. This requires complex and costly, but still not very effective, "qualitative" methodologies such as focus group studies. All of these sophisticated research tools have one goal: to help the advertiser target the desired audience. *That* is what principally determines what appears on our television screens.

How do Canadian media-consumers feel about advertising? In the print media, ads have never been controversial. From their earliest days newspapers have been used to exchange commercial information. Ads were also seen as essential to keep down the prices of mass newspapers and magazines so they could serve the double purpose of creating mass demand for consumer products and teaching new-comers how to live in modern urban Canada. Some students of the history of British journalism argue that the rise of advertising-based newspapers also served the élite's goal of social control by suppressing the previously existing radical press far more effectively than any licensing or taxation laws ever did.[19]

The use of the electronic media for advertising was and to some extent remains more controversial. When radio first developed in Canada and the United States stations were set up primarily by electrical manufacturers and others who used them to attract attention to their principal products. At first there was considerable resistance to using the new medium as a general advertising vehicle, largely because it competed with other advertising media and strategies. For much of the 1920s, then, direct advertising was severely restricted on North American radio; it was allowed only in the daytime "business" hours, for example and banned in the evenings as an unacceptable intrusion into family life.

Eventually, of course — and it did not take long — it became clear that advertising was almost inevitably the only permanent source of sufficient financial support to keep private-enterprise radio afloat. Even after publicly owned broadcasting was introduced in Canada in 1932, advertising contributed a substantial part of its revenues, and it can be argued that only this compromise made government ownership acceptable in many influential business circles. CBC television still earns 20 per cent of its income from advertising. At present, aside from the films at some movie theatres, CBC-owned and -operated radio stations are the only advertisement-free mass media available in Canada. Advertising is to some extent regulated both by the CRTC and by voluntary industry and media guidelines. Advertising of liquor and tobacco and advertising directed at children are the areas which are most controlled, although rules vary depending upon the medium and the province.

North American media consumers seem to accept that advertising comes with the game with little protest. Partly this is because they know no other alternative. Partly it is because they find ads useful sources of information about products. Some, who are less positive about ads, view them as an inevitable tradeoff. One study found that over 84 per cent of Canadians agree that television commercials are necessary because they pay for the free programs provided. Very few viewers seem to be conscious that they pay through higher prices just as surely as they might pay directly under some other system. The same study did show, however, that almost half agreed with the statement that "I'd rather pay money to watch good programs than to put up with all the advertising on television" and almost three-quarters with the statement that "There should be at least one channel on which there is no advertising."[20] Presumably some of the appeal of pay-TV derives from these sentiments.

The survey also revealed something we all know from personal experience — that most people leave the room, switch channels, pick up a magazine or do something else when the commercials come on. About 30 per cent of those questioned said that they often watched the commercials, 38 per cent occasionally, and 32 per cent said that they never watched them. These "avoidance tactics" are, of course, of considerable concern to the advertising industry. They have un-doubtedly become even more common since the survey was done because of the proliferation of remote control channel changers and of VCRs that allow viewers to fast-forward through time-switched programs. The advertising industry has attempted to overcome these problems by a variety of ingenious methods, including product en-dorsements *within* films and TV programs, and by using shorter and more action-packed spots. The networks in turn, beleaguered by falling audience shares, are more receptive to campaigns that tie in product giveaways or theme shows to the interests of advertisers. They have also collaborated to some extent to ensure that commer-cials occur on all channels at the same time.

Advertising is a form of communication and even, some would argue, of culture. Its presence in virtually all our media is integral, not accidental. Its influence and effect are intertwined with the in-fluence and effect of the editorial content it surrounds and pays for. It is thus fundamental not only to the economics of our media but to their cultural impact.

Economists and Culture

The cultural consequences of private-enterprise control of our media have been of some interest to economists. Two main positions are clear. One school, the neoclassical, simply treats cultural goods like any other commodity and holds that the greatest good for the greatest number can be produced only in a free marketplace. According to this viewpoint, any attempts to interfere with the natural law of comparative advantage will cause distortions that will make consum-ers worse off in the end; any sort of protectionism is a cardinal sin. If Canadian-originated cultural goods are unavailable in the Canadian marketplace, they argue, it is because Canadians do not value them enough to pay their price. As Abraham Rotstein (who does not agree with it) summarized this argument:

> Commodities [including cultural commodities] in this perspective are depersonalized, interchangeable and are traded at arm's length. They have no intrinsic significance other than the fact that they have a price tag attached that someone is willing to pay.[21]

From this point of view, the freedom of choice of Canadian consumers is sacred. Economist Stephen Globerman used strong language to indicate how he felt about it in the introduction to his study of the costs of cultural regulation in Canada:

> It can be concluded that government intervention into cultural activities has promoted the growth of cultural production in Canada. Whether it has promoted the general welfare of Canadians is far more questionable, particularly where government intervention has involved the *suppression of the public's right* to consume foreign cultural programming.[22] [italics added]

Even worse, according to Globerman, this sort of intervention serves a nefarious purpose: it transfers income from the general population to a small élite group already above-average in socio-economic status. Thus, he suggests, self-interest is the basis for most of the calls for government regulation and stimulation in the cultural field:

> The main beneficiaries have been and continue to be a select group of performers, producers, and technical personnel, while the bulk of the Canadian population has been burdened with higher prices for the cultural services they consume and with a restricted choice of cultural output.[23]

While Globerman is not totally opposed to all cultural subsidies, he argues that they should be administered only in the form of direct grants so that their results can be better monitored, and that they should be judged by standards of consumption; only those products that prove popular with Canadian audiences merit support. More specifically, Globerman argues that if Canada had a free cultural marketplace cultural output might not be reduced at all, but simply reallocated into the areas where Canadians most appreciate it — for example into local news broadcasts — rather than those decreed important by "coercive government powers."[24] Such a reallocation would be more efficient as well, and therefore allow for greater output with the same resources.

Other economists have been more sensitive to the fact that seemingly irrefutable economic laws have led to a situation that is politically and socially questionable if not actually unacceptable. In the United States the debate has centred around how it is possible to reconcile the freedom of expression enshrined in the First Amendment and assumed to be basic to American democracy with the concentration of media power in the hands of a few that results from the natural workings of another sacred American institution, the free marketplace. While oligopoly may be accepted and even admired for its efficiencies in the automobile industry, it is, perhaps, a different matter when the product being created and transmitted is ideas, information and opinion. There is similar concern about "diversity of voices" in Canada, but here it is heightened by the extent to which our ability to communicate with one another as national citizens is reduced because profit-driven enterprises have such strong incentives to import foreign cultural materials. That issue is of course of little relevance in the United States.

This second group of economists still share many of the preconceptions of the neoclassicists, but they perceive the prevailing situation as an instance of "market failure," that is, a case where the market has failed to produce the "correct" amount of Canadian cultural goods because of the various factors of economies of scale and so on discussed above. They therefore attempt to develop economic rationales to justify governmental intervention that will rectify the marketplace's failure. Because these economists also assume that government interference in the market is a bad thing, elaborate rationalizations must be developed in order to demonstrate that the benefits will outweigh the costs.

The justifications are made on a number of grounds.[25] One might be called the infant-industries argument: that Canadian cultural goods need temporary special protection from normal market forces until they grow strong and self-sufficient. Among other things, it is pointed out that Canada's very large trade deficit in the cultural sector could be reduced if we increased domestic production. Another argument often heard is that cultural industries are particularly labour intensive and therefore contribute a disproportionate amount to the economy and through taxes to government revenues — the multiplier effect. (In 1994-5 the arts and culture sector contributed $29 billion to the Canadian economy.) A third argument in refutation of the neo-classical view is that consumer sovereignty does not really exist in the cultural industries, even in the private marketplace, in part because the newspaper and magazine publishers, broadcasters and other media owners have little direct economic relationship with their consumers, but only with advertisers. Moreover, some of the major media, especially television, are what are known as "public goods," that is, goods for which the use by one consumer does not diminish availability to others. As such, their responsiveness to consumer demand is attenuated.[26] A final economic argument is that cultural products are "merit goods," or goods "that deserve to be fostered, in both their production and public enjoyment, irrespective of how the market may measure costs and benefits — simply because they are meritorious."[27] They have, to use another economists' term, "positive externalities."

Here we get to the crux. Simply put, to everyone but the neoclassicists, cultural industries are not just like other industries. Their product is not just any commodity but is uniquely important in forming consciousness, transmitting information and fostering political debate. These are not economic but cultural functions. Only because the ideas need material vehicles must we get involved in economic questions at all. As Abraham Rotstein has put it, any society encompasses a variety of spheres of activity which often interact but which have different purposes, goals and responsibilities. To examine the mass media through the "market lens" is important, but it reveals only one of the ways they fit into society:

> The market place has no nationality, and does not observe borders and boundaries. Societies on the other hand, have both a nationality and borders. It is to societies rather than to markets that cultural expressions are, in the first instance, addressed and for whom they speak.... We must distinguish, in short, between two things: first, the delivery vehicles for cultural artifacts and the artificial homogeneity which they acquire in the market place and, second, the essential function of culture as the language of a society's existence and continuity.[28]

Culture and the Mass Media

Concentration of ownership and importation of American content, then, are consequences of the fact that most of our media are privately owned and governed by the rules of the marketplace. Why does this matter? Why are oligopoly and foreign content of any more concern than similar patterns in the automobile industry, for example?

The short answer is that the media are one of the principal means by which we learn about our own society. They are also our main source of information and ideas about other societies. The cultural industries are special because they sell products that affect not just what we do but what we think.

It is necessary, however, to be a bit more precise than that. How exactly do the media function in relation to other social organizations? By what processes do they work? What influence do they have to shape or to alter our perceptions? What power do they have to create or to preserve culture? To what extent are they instruments by which one nation can create or reinforce the dependency of another? Only by understanding more fully the role and influence of the media can we determine whether it is justifiable or necessary to interfere with market forces in Canada's cultural industries.

Mass Communications and Culture

"Communication" is a complex concept with many different meanings and connotations. Perhaps the best place to begin is with one of *Webster*'s definitions: "an act or instance of transmitting." This definition is an appropriate brief description of the process of mass communication that occurs via the mass media. A comprehensive and standard definition of mass communication is the one offered by Michael Real in *The Mass-Mediated Society*: "communication which emanates from a single individual or organizational source through electronic or mechanical coding and multiplication of the message to a relatively large, heterogeneous and anonymous audience with only limited and indirect means of feedback."[1] But *Webster*'s also offers another definition of communication: "a process by which information is exchanged between individuals through a common system of symbols, signs or behavior." This definition derives more directly from the root word, the Latin *communico*, meaning to share with another, consult, unite, partake. In this definition the act or process of communication involves a two-way exchange, an interaction. As we shall see, this broader definition of communication is also applicable to the mass media.

The content of the mass media is mass culture. The term "culture" is even more complex and difficult to grasp than communication. In their *Culture: A Critical Review of Concepts and Definitions*, published in 1952, A.L. Kroeber and C. Kluckhohn listed 164 different definitions of culture — and then added their own! In everyday speech, we often use the term to refer to art, literature, architecture, classical music and other self-conscious creative attempts by artists to express their innermost feelings. There is a considerable literature surrounding the effect of the mass media on this type of "high" or élite culture. Much of it condemns the mass media for transmitting a "popular" culture that debases and standardizes artistic forms to appeal to the lowest common denominator of taste. According to this view, high culture challenges, stimulates and creates, while popular culture conforms, lulls and copies. There are also critiques of mass culture from those who believe it has destroyed the indigenous, traditional and local "folk art" traditions of many peoples. On the other hand, as Real points out, both élite and folk art do appear on the mass media, although in somewhat altered forms, and are thereby made accessible to many more people than in their traditional milieus. As such, they, too, become part of what he calls "mass-mediated" culture.

Regardless of how one feels about the effect of the rise of the mass media on high and folk culture, a much larger point needs to be made. What is communicated by the mass media is not simply artistic expression. It is a representation of a society's beliefs, values, traditions — of its whole way of life. The media both reflect our culture and help to mould it; they select and interpret for us. They provide us with a framework of understanding; they produce our reality for us. As Gene Youngblood puts it,

> The [media] for most people most of the time ... specif[y]
> what's real and what's not (existence), what's important and
> what's not (priorities), what's good and what's bad (values) and
> what's related to what else and how (relations).[2]

Anthropologists have traditionally defined culture as "that complex whole which includes knowledge, belief, art, morals, law, custom and any other capabilities and habits acquired by man as a member of society."[3] Culture is the glue that holds any society together, because it is the domain in which the symbols, ideas, myths and attitudes of individuals are formed. Without the bonds created by culture, a society cannot exist, because culture explains where we have come from, how the world works and where we may go. It is our "meaning-generating" system. Both at the individual and the collective levels, it forms our identity, it is our common language. According to Abraham Rotstein:

> Culture as 'language,' used in the larger sense of the term, is
> thus one of the broad, if not the broadest feature of the unity
> and coherence of a society. It is the essential binding feature
> without which any semblance of orderly discourse and interac-
> tion would disappear.[4]

It is because this "constructing" culture is formed by communication among the members of the society, and because a significant proportion of our communication these days (although by no means all) occurs via the mass media, that studying them is so important.

> As media institutions are among the constituting elements of
> our age, mediatization — that is to say, the range of production
> and reception practices that media foster, as well as the particu-
> lar way in which they transform reality while producing it —
> lies at the heart of social, collective, intercultural, and interna-
> tional relations. At every level, from the local to the global,
> contemporary culture is increasingly subject to mediatization.[5]

Theories of Mass Communication

Scholars first became interested in the mass media in the years immediately after the First World War.[6] From the beginning, their main concern was about the effects of mass communications on individual audience members. Early studies determined that the mass media were an enormously powerful social force, a "bullet" or "needle" that penetrated and transformed minds. Partly this conclusion was the result of observation: the evident popularity and rapid spread of mass newspapers, magazines, movies and radio through the application of new technology in the early twentieth century; the effectiveness of the propaganda utilized by many governments during the First World War; and especially, Hitler's very successful exploitation of the media in Germany in the 1930s. It was also based upon the prevailing assumption among sociologists of the day that industrialization and urbanization had created a "mass society" of rootless and alienated people, no longer bound together by traditional church, family and community ties, and therefore easy prey for manipulators.

Beginning in the late 1940s, and continuing for a couple of decades, a number of researchers mainly in the United States began to test these conclusions with empirical studies to determine whether media messages really do change people's minds. The conclusion reached, in general, was that they do not. Experiments indicated quite decisively that individuals are very selective in what they understand and remember from the media. Rather than being passive "victims" of media manipulators, audiences are active participants in the communication process. Depending upon their own backgrounds, beliefs and predispositions, as well as the immediate influence of family and friends, audience members filter out or alter those messages they do not wish to hear. While researchers of this school did not completely deny media effects, they argued that they were minimal, complex and difficult to measure.

The recognition by researchers that individual audience members have some control over how they absorb media messages was a useful corrective to the earlier assumption of passivity and powerlessness. But it also went too far, for it seemed to suggest that the media have so little influence that we do not need to concern ourselves about them. Common sense, not to mention the ongoing faith of the advertising industry concretely demonstrated by the expenditure of millions of dollars a year in the media, suggested otherwise. The principal problem was that much of this early empirical work had been based upon the false premise that one could demonstrate media influence only by showing how it changed people's minds. On the contrary, the next generation of scholars argued, the major influence of the media is not in altering but in reinforcing, consolidating and fortifying values and attitudes, especially over a long period of time. One well-known example of these points comes from a study done in the early 1970s comparing the reaction of groups of viewers in a Midwestern American community and London, Ontario, to the racial and ethnic jokes on the popular sitcom "All in the Family." The researchers found that viewers who had prior attitudes of high prejudice admired the Archie Bunker character more and did not perceive the show as a satire on bigotry. They also tended to watch the program more than those who scored for low prejudice. The researchers concluded that their findings suggested that "the program is more likely reinforcing prejudice and racism than combatting it."[7]

All of this early debate was based on what is often called the "transportation" model of media, that is, an assumption that the media primarily function as transmitters, sending messages from a source to an audience. Most researchers of this era focussed on Harold Lasswell's famous sequence: "Who says what in which channel to whom with what effect?" They examined producers, content, media, audiences and impact as relatively discrete entities. Most, but not all of them, also worked within the liberal-pluralist perspective.

According to the liberal-pluralist view, society is formed of many competing groups and interests, none of them permanently predominant. The media comprise one of these groups, reasonably autonomous from all the others, but with a special role as the forum in which contending economic and political viewpoints battle it out. The professionals who actually create media content have a considerable amount of independence, and govern themselves according to their own codes of ethics and professional behaviour. Most particularly, they strive for objectivity and fairness in their presentation of facts, and a clear separation between facts and opinion. While these professionals have power over their audiences, it is the power of the gatekeeper or the agenda-setter only. From this viewpoint, audiences are seen as capable of making their own choices. They have considerable control and influence by virtue of their ability to choose to consume media content or not. When they do opt to receive the message, they can accept it, accommodate it to their previous beliefs, challenge it or reject it. According to this school of thought, then, the media are "mirrors of reality," the neutral channels whereby reality is made more widely known. Some who work within this paradigm agree, however, that simply because the media are so interconnected with the prevailing social system they serve primarily to reinforce it, to preserve the status quo. This is generally not seen to be problematic, however; on the contrary, it is viewed as a useful and necessary contribution toward maintaining order in a complex and rapidly evolving society.

Not all the early theorists were liberal-pluralists doing quantitative empirical research, however; some of them were Marxists. The latter group saw the media as a principal route by which the values, goals and propaganda of the ruling class are transmitted to the ordinary people. They noted that most if not all media institutions are in the hands of monopoly capitalists and argued that journalists and other professionals working in the field have little autonomy. From this perspective, the media's messages consistently convey assumptions, attitudes and interpretive frameworks that support, or at least do not challenge, the interests of the dominant class. Messages that do call for fundamental change are weeded out or made to appear deviant. While audiences may not necessarily accept everything they hear or see from the class-biased media, lacking alternative avenues of expression they are unable to do much about it. According to this view, then, the media are not mirrors but "megaphones" by which ruling-class ideas are amplified and dispersed.

Beginning in the 1960s and continuing to the present, some alternative and inter-related sets of ideas for understanding the functions of the media have developed — the cultural, neo-Marxist and critical models. Communications scholar James Carey has suggested that while the notion of communications as transportation has tended to dominate in American research, in Europe (including Britain), the concept of communications primarily as culture has won wider acceptance (as it has to some extent in Canada, where the influence of Harold Innis has been important). To those who take the cultural-studies tack, communication is ritual, mythology and art, a "process through which a shared culture is created, modified and transformed."[8] "A ritual view of communication is directed not toward the extension of messages in space but toward the maintenance of society in time."[9] Carey gives an example of how the newspaper may be studied from the two different perspectives. Those scholars who assume that communication is transmission look at such issues as how news is selected, the effect it has on its readers, and how the newspaper functions within a given social structure. The scholar who emphasizes the ritual view sees the process of reading a newspaper as more like attending a mass. Through the paper, a particular view of the world is portrayed and confirmed; the reader does not receive information but watches a drama of contending forces in the world. The newspaper does not have effects or functions as such; rather it offers a presentation of the form, order and tone of the world as it is.[10]

For those who perceive communication to be primarily a cultural ritual, then, the media act as the builders of community, creating the common outlooks that form the basis for a shared consciousness. No longer is the audience an anonymous mass of isolated individuals, but rather it is composed of groups held together by cultural cement, interacting with one another and with the media to continue to transform that culture. According to one prominent proponent, Raymond Williams, normally there are at least three cultures coexisting in any society: the "dominant" culture expressing the mainstream view of those with social and political power, the "residual" culture still maintaining a certain cohesiveness from traditional cultural forms, and the "emergent" culture, challenging the dominant and struggling to replace it.[11]

In general, those who hold this view of the media have tended to a more inclusive, complex and critical study of their dynamics. Unlike earlier Marxists who simply assumed that because the media are owned by monopoly capitalists they send capitalist messages, more recent scholars examine in detail how the institutional structure works, including not only the inter-relationships of power in the whole society but also how this is translated into television programs and newspaper copy by way of organizational hierarchies and professional practices. Critical theorists do not see the media as crude agents of propaganda but rather as actors within a complex social process; nevertheless, they conclude that the media do act to maintain social consensus, to deflect challenges against those with economic power and generally to support the existing order. As Stuart Hall put it, "We can speak, then, only of the *tendency* of the media — but it is a systematic tendency, not an incidental feature — to reproduce the ideological field of a society in such a way as to reproduce, also, its structure of domination."[12] In this view, the media do not simply reflect the status quo but help to make it; the very fact that they are generally perceived to be autonomous and impartial only increases their power.

Recent scholarship also examines in a much more precise and audience-centred manner than the old school of "content analysis" how messages are created and interpreted. Most influential here is the approach often called "representation of texts," a development from structural linguistics and semiotics. Put simply, semioticians study "signs," that is, representations of objects or events, in the context of "texts" which may be anything from gestures to paintings to billboards. They examine how the text is produced (encoded) and interpreted (decoded) but more important they study its meaning (or "preferred reading") in the widest, most connotative sense. Their analysis of a media message is widely embracing: while focussing on the text itself they argue that it can be understood only in the fuller symbolic and cultural context in which both those who produce and those who "read" it exist. This approach also allows for questions not only about the use for which the message is intended or to which it is put but also about its moral and aesthetic characteristics. Such a study is not quantitative or empirical but much more theoretical and intuitive.

In summary, while mass-communications scholars have developed many different analyses of the mass media in the past fifty or sixty years, the direction of current scholarship emphasizes certain key points. First, the mass media are rooted in our society and in the power-relationships within it. One cannot understand their function without examining the political, technological and economic infrastructures within which they operate. Secondly, the mass media are themselves institutions acting within the larger society; one must therefore also examine the various constraints and professional practices operative within each medium. Thirdly, a subtle and wide-ranging analysis of the signs and symbols inherent in the content of the media can reveal the reciprocal process by which producers and audiences "negotiate" meanings on an on-going basis. Michael Real writes:

> As a virtually omnipresent symbolic form, mass-mediated culture expresses and determines human descriptions of life and definitions of reality. Research and analysis ... establish that mass-mediated culture has the power (a) to shape behavior and beliefs; (b) to determine aesthetic taste in cultural and artistic matters; (c) to maintain or modify the arrangement of society; and, through all of these, (d) to play a part in ordering or disordering personal, group, and international life.[13]

The inter-relationship among all these functions is crucial. The scholars who emphasize media power and domination often downplay both the interpretive role of the audience and symbolic content. Those who concentrate only on the diversity of audience response frequently ignore the extent to which the meaning of the text is influenced by the economic and social structure within which it is produced. The best studies today are those that recognize that the media must be studied simultaneously as institutions, as texts and as social discourse.

The Media and Dependency

No matter how sophisticated and theoretical it became, most of the mass-communications research up to the 1970s concentrated on how the media functioned within the borders of a single country.[14] The one major exception was a group of American scholars who theorized that the media had the power to act as agents of progress and modernization (and American values) in newly independent colonies in Asia and Africa.[15] Beginning in the late 1960s some scholars began to turn a more critical eye to the role played by western media, especially American, in the non-western countries (some prefer the terms developing countries or South). Their interest derived partly from the general concern with western/non-western relations that arose during the Vietnam War era and partly from the growing number of objections coming from the developing countries themselves about media penetration from external sources. These objections in turn derived from a need to explain the paradox that the political freedom achieved by former colonies during the 1960s had not lessened their dependency.

Media "imperialism" began during the last great scramble for colonial possessions in the late nineteenth century. (The word imperialism suggests actual territorial conquest, while dependency suggests economic control despite ostensible sovereignty. Thomas McPhail has coined the graphic term "electronic colonialism.") The European powers' need for better political, military and especially economic information from around the world spurred the development of telegraphs, underwater cables, wireless telegraph and radio and the establishment of two great international news agencies, Reuters (British) and Havas (French; now replaced by Agence France-Presse). As the United States rose to world-power status before and during the Second World War the American agencies Associated Press and United Press International successfully challenged the domination of Reuters and Havas in international news gathering and dissemination.

Today these four agencies dominate world news. Their correspondents in cities all over the globe gather local news which is then selected and edited for distribution to subscribing newspapers and broadcasters. Some 80 to 90 per cent of the international news flow passes through these agencies; all of it is gathered, sifted, ordered and written by agency staffers for western consumption. Although they contain the majority of the world's population, news from the countries of the non-western world constitutes only 10 or 20 per cent of the total. The information that does originate in developing countries is biased by the definition of "news" common to the western media and tends to focus on disasters, riots, coups and other dramatic and often negative events. Not far from the truth was a *Village Voice* cartoon showing a TV set blaring: "Coming up next on the news, terrifying, inexplicable events occurring in far-away places, presented without historical or sociological context!"[16]

In the past fifty years entertainment has also become an international commodity, with resulting cultural, economic and technological ramifications. From the 1920s on the American film and television industries in particular have by a combination of money, volume and clever tactics blasted their way onto the screens of the world. By the late 1940s American films garnered more than 70 per cent of the audiences in countries as diverse as South Africa, Brazil, Thailand, Persia, Turkey and Portugal. While the United States now produces only about 6 or 7 per cent of the world's films, these movies still attract about half the total audiences. Similarly, an average of about one-third of the programs appearing on TV screens around the globe in the late twentieth century were imported from the United States. (The three main American networks themselves carry only 2 per cent imported shows, the smallest proportion in the world; most of that is Spanish-language material.) In addition, American advertising agencies have cooperated with or bought out local agencies in major cities in both developed and developing countries, and their clients, mainly American-owned transnational corporations, have become the major advertisers on commercial broadcasting channels in many nations. Finally, not the least among the media products spread abroad has been technology: the equipment and expert practices necessary to establish modern media systems.

According to most recent scholars, exposure to western media has had detrimental effects on developing countries. For one thing, the creation of demand for advanced consumer products advertised through the westernized media has skewed economic priorities. "The flow of media exports acts as a kind of ideological prerequisite for the flow of other material exports."[17] Exposure to western media has also helped exaggerate material expectations and increase resentment over inequalities, thus destabilizing international relations. But it is not just western products that are sold on the mass media of other countries. If the cultural analysis presented in the first section of this chapter has any validity, so are western values, institutions and behaviour that may be very inappropriate for other cultures. According to those who view mass communications as part of a socio-political whole, then, the mass media of the industrialized countries are integral to the political and economic activities that place non-western countries in a dependent position. Mustapha Masmoudi, one of the principal critics of media dependency, writes:

> Advertising, magazines and television programs are today so many instruments of cultural domination and acculturation, transmitting to the developing countries messages which are harmful to their cultures, contrary to their values, and detrimental to their development aims and efforts.[18]

The unbalanced flow of news and entertainment via the mass media is not the only concern. It is a cliché today to suggest we live in the "information age," but there is a real truth underlying the phrase. The collection and distribution of demographic, resource, financial, market and other information has become central to the functioning of the transnational corporations and of all the world's economies. In that context, the issue of how the world's electromagnetic spectrum and geostationary orbits will be divided for different kinds of communications uses has already become a critical aspect of economic and foreign policy for both the major powers and for the emerging countries, as has the question of transborder computer-data and Internet flows.

The picture just painted is in stark black-and-white; the addition of some shades of grey is, however, necessary. One qualification is that by far the majority of exports of film, television programs and so on from the developed world go to other western nations, not to the developing countries. Moreover, although the United States has the largest news agencies and widest international distribution of film and television products, it is by no means the only exporter of culture. As the European Union, for example, consolidates its economic and cultural industry policies, world media flows will probably increasingly involve both rivalries and inter-relationships among the developed nations. Another factor is that in the developing nations, distribution and language barriers restrict the consumption of west-

ernized media for the most part to the urban élites (which are, however, disproportionately influential). It is also important to remember
that many non-western governments and élites have welcomed western media technology and content because they have perceived its
utility to their own goals of hastening modernization and achieving
national integration. Varying inter-ethnic and class relationships
within non-western countries have led to different perceptions and
uses of western media. In other words, the situation is much more
complex than simple "imperialism" and "dependency" language describes.

Equally significant according to some scholars is the fact that
many of the dominant media and advertising interests in the world
today are really transnational enterprises, not necessarily espousing
the goals of any one nation. Is it "American cultural imperialism"
when millions of Chinese viewers receive Australian-born Rupert
Murdoch's Star satellite signals? Maybe. Certainly the values of
capitalism and consumerism are conveyed whatever the ownership.
But the situation is not as straightforward as it once seemed.

Finally, as we have already seen, it is generally accepted by
mass-communications scholars that audiences select and interpret
media messages according to their own context and experiences.
Non-western audiences are certainly no more — and probably less
— the isolated alienated victims of media manipulation than are
western audiences. The greater cultural differences provide a fine-
meshed filtering screen that enables demystification and resistance.
One example of this point comes from a study that compared how
three different groups of people living in Israel perceived certain
episodes of the popular American serial "Dallas." Elihu Katz and
Tamara Liebes demonstrated that very different observations and
conclusions were drawn by peoples of different cultures. One scene,
for example, showed Sue Ellen Ewing moving in with her lover and
his father. To a group of Israeli Arabs who watched this episode her
action was so morally repugnant that they simply blocked it out;
when asked what Sue Ellen had done, they told the researcher that
she had gone to live with her father.[19] Canadian research into how
the Inuit responded to the introduction of southern television in the
1970s showed similar results. One study suggested, for example, that
young male Inuit viewers "synthesized" the divergent cultural traditions by dressing in black leather jackets and boots like The Fonz to
go out hunting.[20] While studies of this type have been dismissed by
media imperialism theorists as politically motivated (one suggested,

for example, that Katz and Liebes's work on "Dallas" was accorded substantial coverage in the New York *Times* only because it was seen to refute charges of American cultural imperialism)[21] and for ignoring the central issue of power, they do nevertheless suggest that a more subtle analysis of the precise significance of international media flow is necessary.

From a slightly different point of view, other commentators have pointed to considerable evidence that despite the long-term and massive penetration of western media, the world today is ideologically, ethnically, religiously and nationally not only pluralist but increasingly divergent. Simultaneously two different cultural phenomena seem to be occurring: one the homogenization of culture along American lines ("McWorld"), the other a resurgence of "tribalism."[22] While the first cannot be totally resisted, ironically it has the "perverse effect" of fuelling the second. Moreover, it is argued, this process is both valid and valuable; all countries need the stimulation of outside ideas, and they can learn much from the United States — including how to use its own methods to empower themselves. This particular argument, like that of the "Dallas" example, rests on a profound belief in the audience, a recognition of the great pleasure that many generations of people around the world have derived from American popular culture — and a deep disagreement with those who, in arguing cultural imperialism, deny to audiences anywhere in the world the intelligence, perspicacity, critical spirit and imagination to perceive the foreign as alien and to take from it only what they will.[23]

All these qualifications and counter-arguments having been stated, however, it is still not surprising that the western and commercial predominance over the world's news flow, entertainment programming, advertising industry and information collection has been viewed with great concern in non-western countries. This domination is generally seen as part of a greater economic, political and military imbalance that afflicts the developing world and threatens peace. Objections to this situation have been coalescing since at least 1973 when the non-aligned nations at a conference in Algiers called specifically for a New International Economic Order (NIEO) and a New International Information Order (the more commonly used term now is New World Information and Communication Order or NWICO) as corollary steps towards decolonization.

After several years of increasingly polarized debate, in 1977 UNESCO, the United Nations agency for educational, scientific and cultural matters, commissioned a sixteen-member international group, headed by Sean MacBride of Ireland, to examine "communication problems" on a global scale. The MacBride Commission's report, published in 1980 under the title *Many Voices, One World*, crystallized many of the issues just described. While the commission's attempts to register dissent and multiplicity of views resulted in a complex and qualified document, certain general points may be made about its conclusions. As its title suggests, the report argued that there should be more diversity in the viewpoints available about global issues. The commission, with some caveats from its American and Canadian members, deplored the constraints on the media imposed by commercialization, advertiser-financing and concentration. It also condemned, however, censorship (the Soviet delegate dissenting) and criticized tendencies toward narrow national parochialism. Most important, the commission recognized that an imbalance existed in global communications and information distribution, and called for their "democratization" both inter- and intra-nationally.

The NWICO and Freedom of Expression

The attack on media imperialism and the call for a New World Information and Communication Order were received in the western democracies, and especially the United States, with considerable hostility. Much of the controversy focussed around the issues of the "free flow" of information, freedom of expression and freedom of the press (the terms are often used interchangeably).

The four-theory model of the press developed in the 1950s by F.S. Siebert, T. Peterson and W. Schramm helps illuminate this debate.[24] Siebert *et al.* began their analysis with what they called the "authoritarian" press, the traditional system in which the government either owned all the presses, or subjected other publishers to close government supervision (for example in Britain by the licensing system established under Henry VIII and later by seditious libel laws and stamp taxes). In this arrangement, the media were required to support established authority and were subject to economic sanctions, censorship or even criminal penalties if they attacked that authority or deviated from its policies. Essentially, they were subordinate to the broader social interest as defined by the state.

Beginning with the battles of seventeenth-century British publishers to free themselves from official control, and enshrined particularly in the First Amendment to the American Constitution, there next arose the "libertarian" theory of the press. According to this idea, any individual should be able to publish his or her ideas freely subject only to restrictions in cases where other individuals might be harmed thereby. This theory has its premises in other beliefs we also associate with the liberal-democratic state: individualism, reason, popular sovereignty and laissez-faire economics. The assumption is that out of the open competition among ideas freely expressed, the best will prevail. The ideal of objectivity, most specifically the belief that the job of the journalist is to report "only the facts," is also now central. A very important extension of the libertarian theory has been its use to justify the private ownership of the media and freedom from government interference in the marketplace. The assumption is that advertiser-supported media are the vehicles for free expression while state-supported media are not. In the United States in particular, it is commonly believed that in adherence to this principle virtually no restrictions should be placed on the activities of privately owned cultural enterprises, including their right to export their products around the world.

In the twentieth century, culminating with the Hutchins Commission in the U.S. in the 1940s, there developed a third concept of the press, "social responsibility." This idea originated in the recognition that freedom of the press from governmental interference had in fact resulted in concentrated ownership in the hands of a small powerful socio-economic élite possessed of near-absolute freedom to propound its own view of the world. The rise of broadcasting also provided a stimulus to this reorientation, because it was recognized that great power was granted to the few given the privilege of using scarce space on the electromagnetic spectrum. The Hutchins Commission argued that a free press must also be a responsible press, reflecting the views of all citizens and dominated by none. It recommended that press councils and other measures be instituted to ensure that the press remained fair as well as free, although it stopped short of advocating direct government intervention.

The fourth concept of the press identified by Siebert and his colleagues is the "totalitarian" approach, primarily as practised at that time in the Soviet Union. In that system, the assumption was that the Communist party embodied the highest will of the people, and that the primary task of the press was therefore not only to represent but to promote the party's viewpoint. State ownership, censorship and other means of strict control of opinion and information were justified in the name of the people and the state.

These four theories of the press, particularly the first two, set the pattern for the debate that developed in the late 1970s over the concept of the NWICO. The western media in general and the United States in particular defended the libertarian view of a press free of governmental control and financed by private enterprise; they were suspicious that the NWICO involved authoritarian or totalitarian control of the media, and that Soviet manipulation lay behind the demands of the non-western countries. The opponents of the NWICO expressed great concern that virtually all the solutions proposed to rectify the international information imbalance involved state intervention in the communications sector, including strict regulation or even exclusion of foreign media ownership and content to make room for domestic voices to speak, and in some cases prohibition of dissent. They charged that collective goals had taken precedence over individual freedoms.

Yet, non-western proponents of the new communications order and the concept of "developmental" journalism (considered by some scholars a fifth approach to add to Siebert's list) did not see their position as authoritarian or totalitarian. They argued that authoritarianism is a negative and arbitrary form of media control, whereas what they advocated was positive, aimed at encouraging the national autonomy and cultural identity of dependent societies by reducing external domination. They were not striving to silence, they claimed, but to allow more voices expression. According to the NWICO view, there is no such thing as "objective" journalism; its supporters claimed that the western media in professing this ideal in fact were simply serving the economic and political interests of *their* own societies. Proponents of the NWICO reject a western press that dominates in the name of "freedom" in favour of a better-balanced world press that supports national sovereignty. As one scholar summed it up:

> The emerging LDC's [less developed countries] maintain that the preservation of a unique and healthy cultural and national identity and the right as autonomous independent nations to pursue self-determined social, economic, political and communication goals override the international principle of free flow of information.[25]

These concepts were and for the most part remain anathema to the western democracies. Thus, a polarization occurred over these issues between 1973 and 1984, and many observers believe it was an important factor in the American decision to withdraw from UNESCO in the latter year. The United Kingdom subsequently withdrew as well. As a result, the only concrete outcome of the MacBride Report has been the creation of the International Program for the Development of Communications (IPDC), a clearing-house and to a lesser extent a funding agency to aid developing countries and regions to improve their own communications systems. While the rhetoric has cooled since 1985, especially within UNESCO, which under new leadership has pretty well abandoned NWICO in favour of a new pragmatism, the issues remain deeply divisive and continue to affect a wide range of negotiations regarding the development of journalism, satellites, telecommunications and transborder data-flow in the IPDC and such other bodies as the OECD and the International Telecommunications Union. One current concern of UNESCO, for example, is the disadvantage of poor countries and their poorer citizens in gaining access to the information now available via the Internet, as well as the potential domination of the Internet by the English language.

As mentioned above, however, the future debate on all these issues will take place in a much different international context; analyses will have to be more subtle and sophisticated, taking into account not only the evolution of the world's power structures, but also class and maybe even gender. Some of the more thoughtful supporters of NWICO, for example, now recognize that it was never a mass movement, but one which was supported by certain élites in non-western nations for their own reasons.[26]

One of the most interesting recent developments is the increased apprehension in Europe about the inflow of American entertainment media, and the replication of NWICO arguments from a part of the world which traditionally had only limited concern about these issues. The context of course is not only the massive structural changes in Europe in the last decade — the disintegration of the Soviet Union, the independence of its former satellites, the reunification of Germany, the creation of the European Community (now the European Union) — but also, more specifically within the media field, the move to deregulation and privatization, especially in broadcasting. The increased commercialization of European television and the multiplication of channels caused by the sanctioning of satellites and cable systems resulted in the 1980s in a marked acceleration in the import of inexpensive American programs. In 1988, for example,

American programs took up about 28 per cent of the hours on European TV stations. "American media imperialism" thus became a hot
issue in Europe (and especially in France), despite its relatively
well-rooted and stable cultures whose audiences have traditionally
preferred domestic media products. In 1989 the EC announced a
commitment to ensure that European programs be exchanged freely
within the community and that the majority of programs broadcast
"where practicable" be European; American officials proclaimed that
they were much perturbed by this "absurd effort to regulate public
taste."[27]

Canada's position in this whole debate has been a curiously am-
bivalent one. Canadians generally accept the libertarian ideals of
freedom to create, to consume and to sell information and entertainment. The Constitution Act of 1982 indeed enshrined for the first
time in Section 2(b) of the Charter of Rights and Freedoms our
equivalent to the American First Amendment, guaranteeing "freedom of thought, belief, opinion and expression, including freedom
of the press and other media of communication" (although this is
subject to the notwithstanding clause). Canada has generally backed
the U.S. defence of freedom of information in UNESCO discussions,
then, because we share the concern for freedom of the press, because
we are a part of the western bloc, and also probably because some
Canadian media interests have their eyes on world markets for technology and programming. At the same time, however, as we have
already seen, Canada has been the single nation in the world most
vulnerable to the effects of penetration by American cultural industries, and it has adopted various protectionist measures in response.
Canada consequently supported the European move toward quotas,
although it did lobby vigorously to ensure that Canadian co-productions would be counted as "European." Canada has also taken a lead
in a new group called the International Network on Cultural Policy,
which includes countries such as Brazil, Egypt, Britain, Sweden,
Ukraine, France, China and Senegal (but not, of course, the United
States), and has as its mission "to discuss the importance of sustain-
ing national cultures in the face of globalization and to promote
cooperation on common cultural objectives."[28]

A number of commentators on the international imbalance prob-
lem have noted Canada's anomalous position on these matters.[29]
Anthony Smith put it best in his 1980 book *The Geopolitics of
Information: How Western Culture Dominates the World*:

The culturally and politically debilitating effects of media dependence are perhaps most eloquently illustrated by taking an
example not from the non-aligned or developing countries but
from within the developed world itself.... [Canada] has con-
ceded the right of free flow and has suffered the consequences.... No country in the world probably is more
completely committed to the practice of free flow in its culture
and no country is more completely its victim.... [Canada's]
history indicates that dependence is far harder to escape from
than colonialism; it grows with the sophistication of technology
and administration and it demonstrates the way in which the
liberal doctrines of a dominant society are not necessarily liberal in their impact upon a dominated society.... It is extremely
difficult for a society to practise free flow of media and enjoy
a national culture at the same time — unless it happens to be
the United States of America.[30]

With the general pattern of the global issues in mind, let us turn to
look at the debate within Canada about how protection and enhance-
ment of our national culture can be reconciled with private enterprise
and freedom of information.

The Pros and Cons of Canadian Cultural Nationalism

The first significant expression of English-Canadian cultural nationalism vis-à-vis the American mass media erupted in the 1920s. Peaks
occurred again in the 1960s and most recently at the time of the
intense discussion about the Free Trade Agreement with the United
States. Canadians have by no means been of one mind on this issue.
Let us examine the various positions taken over the years by the
device of a mock debate.

*Resolved: "Government intervention is necessary to preserve
Canadian culture endangered by the Americanization of our
mass media."*

Affirmative:

A nation must have its own communication links, specifically control
of its own mass media, to facilitate the formation and expression of
its own culture. Without that binding culture, the nation will disap-

pear. As the Report of the O'Leary Royal Commission on Publications put it:

> Socrates' saying that the unexamined life is unfit to be lived is applicable to a nation as to an individual. A society or community, deprived of searching criticism of its own, among its own and by its own, has within it seeds of decay.... It may be claimed — claimed without much challenge — that the communications of a nation are as vital to its life as its defences, and should receive at least as great a measure of national protection.[31]

Margaret Atwood made the same point in her well-known study of Canadian literary themes, *Survival*: "For the members of a country or a culture, shared knowledge of their place, their here, is not a luxury but a necessity. Without that knowledge we will not survive."[32]

A more recent expression of the same injunction comes from Paul Audley, one of Canada's foremost cultural industry analysts:

> The primary significance of magazines, books, films, and other cultural works is social, cultural, and political. Communities and nations whose past is not reflected in publications, broadcast programs, films, and video and audio productions are as handicapped as individuals affected with amnesia. Societies whose current realities are not adequately explored, reflected, debated, and contested through works that are widely available ... will increasingly become democratic in name only....[33]

The economic realities, however, dictate that as long as our media remain private enterprises driven by market forces, they will be filled with American material or actually owned by Americans. But every hour or page devoted to foreign content on our mass media is one less available for Canadians to speak to each other. When Canadian voices are heard, they do say different things in different ways than American voices. Although regrettably not enough research has yet been undertaken in this area, various studies show that there is an identifiable cultural difference between English-Canadian and American media content, not only in the selection of different subjects for news and entertainment, but in the tone and values conveyed — Canadian-produced television programs are noticeably less violent, for example.[34] Even those who tend to deplore Canadian cultural nationalism admit this fact.[35] The only possible protection of this unique expression is government regulation to require Canadian ownership and content of our media, or even actual government ownership, run on the principle of public service rather than profit. Canadian historian A.R.M. Lower wrote in 1953:

> There is no doubt in my mind that if we Canadians allow television to pass under American control and with American programs providing the determinative element in the items offered, we may as well sooner or later shut up shop: our future will be American. Persons who deny this are blind when they are not worse. They were characterized in Parliament as "virtually traitors." With this description I agree. It is not a matter of public vs. private ownership — at least that is a secondary aspect of the controversy. The point is that private ownership means American control. No amount of subterfuge can whittle that statement away.[36]

There are also some very practical reasons why we should encourage a more Canadianized mass media. Canadian creative artists need opportunities to express themselves. They also need employment. Being labour intensive, the cultural industries create a disproportionate number of jobs and enhance tax revenues. Canadian companies also require Canadian media on which to place advertisements for their products. Both the cultural and the manufactured goods of Canada need protection from the economic might of the United States.

Canada is an economic dependent of the United States. Much of our manufacturing sector is American-owned, and in the future under the Free Trade Agreement and NAFTA our service sectors will be increasingly integrated. The only way to preserve our independence as a nation is to retain control of our communications sector, so we can continue to form bonds with one another rather than with Americans. That is why it was so important that cultural industries be left out of the free-trade negotiations. We run the risk of our values and beliefs and attitudes becoming indistinguishable from the American.

While Quebec is somewhat protected from American culture by language, even in that province there are reasons for great alarm about the penetration of American television, popular music and films. Not even a different language is strong enough to act as a natural barrier against the mass-media giant of the world — our next-door neighbour.

Canadian-born Harvard economist John Kenneth Galbraith wrote a number of years ago: "If I were still a practising as distinct from an advisory Canadian, I would be much more concerned about who owned the newspapers, magazines and television stations than about who owned the factories."[37] It is essential that Canada practise "defensive expansionism" by using the government to restrain and counteract the American presence in order to preserve and promote the cultural expression of our distinct sovereignty.

Negative:

The large presence of American popular culture in Canadian society, and particularly on our mass media, is the product of historical development; it is a natural phenomenon. The first large group of English-speaking Canadians, the Loyalists, were Americans, and they founded in English Canada a North American culture that is common to both countries. Since the nineteenth century most Canadians have largely adhered to American values such as individualism and free enterprise; our society is basically American in its shape and outlook, and therefore our culture is too. "The popular arts in Canada have always been foreign, never alien."[38] The border is imaginary.

The evidence is overwhelming that Canadians not only enjoy but actually prefer American popular culture. One English-speaking Quebecker told a surveyor in 1938: "I subscribe to a number of American periodicals, including the *Red Book* and *Cosmopolitan* — all light reading. I find Canadian magazines so very dull and uninteresting...."[39] More recently a Montreal newspaper columnist put the point more colourfully:

> Politicians take note: If we wanted Canadian content, dammit, we'd watch the *Beachcombers*. Will you clowns please stop forcing us to watch boring drivel made by your greedy and clamorous friends in the "cultural community"! Go away and leave us in peace to watch *Miami Vice*![40]

When Canadian content (Cancon) rules were imposed on television and radio stations Canadians complained loudly — especially those who lived too far from the border to be able to receive American TV. The general desire for direct access to American television is the principal reason for the fact that Canada has one of the highest rates of cable penetration in the world. As well, a number of polls have shown that Canadians consistently believe that American TV programs are superior to their own.[41] No one forces American television, magazines, movies, newspaper comic strips or popular music on Canadians — they have shown how much they want these products by their willingness to purchase them in large numbers. Former CRTC chairman John Meisel put it well: "Canadians regard their right to watch American TV programming with the same passion as Americans regard their right to bear arms."[42]

The issue is really one of freedom: first, freedom of expression and free access to the marketplace for all producers of cultural products no matter what their nationality, and secondly, freedom for all Canadian consumers to purchase what they want without censorship. Any interference in the natural functioning of the marketplace for cultural products, whether by regulation or by public ownership, is an interference not only with the most efficient and productive economic system but with the principle of freedom of speech fundamental to democracy. The consumer must be sovereign; the wishes of ordinary Canadians must not be ignored.

It is also clear that most of the measures introduced so far by the Canadian government to counteract the natural desires of ordinary Canadians have been undertaken in the self-interest of a small élite that will benefit personally from rules and regulations imposing Canadian culture. If their products were truly valued by Canadians, they would be purchased. Instead, Canadian cultural producers have disdained anything "popular" as "American" and have lost touch with their own audiences. Because this élite is articulate and has access to the media, however, it has managed to convince Canadians that its interests are theirs. It claims the authority to define Canadian cultural goods as morally superior without addressing the issue of quality or admitting that other Canadians have the right to different cultural tastes. Attempts to interfere with the marketplace are thus not only economically inefficient but unpopular and self-serving. Quite simply, "The Cancon policy involves the coercion of the many ... to provide benefits to a few...."[43] "Cancon ... has been exactly that: a con game for Canadians."[44]

Not only cultural but economic élites have benefited disproportionately from nationalist cultural policies. Large corporate empires have been built behind a wall of legislation protecting Canadian firms from real competition. Arbitrary rules about subsidizing Canadian content have not guaranteed that Canadian stories will be told, only that Canadians will get the work. Worse, they have encouraged practices like setting up shell companies and hiring "fake Canadians" that are, if not corrupt, certainly sleazy.[45] As Matthew Fraser put it in his recent work on the media and the "digital frontier": "The language of cultural nationalism — notably vis-à-vis the American leviathan — has become a necessary illusion conveniently exploited to legitimize the ambitions of state-protected Canadian business interests that, in fact, are more attached to the rewards of global markets than to the ambitions of so-called Canadian 'cultural sovereignty.'"[46]

Another extremely negative result of the nationalist approach to culture has been the centralization of media control in Toronto and Montreal and the consequent destruction of regional and ethnic identities. Far from creating national unity, these endeavours have exacerbated tensions within Canada. Many people in many regions, and especially those in Quebec, believe that the excessive focus on creating nationalism through federal cultural institutions has ignored their points of view. The emphasis on a national struggle against American culture has diverted attention from the fact that what Canada really needs is more inter-regional and inter-language communication.[47] Canada is becoming more, not less, decentralized, and media regulations that force "pan-Canadianism" are simply out of step with reality. Threats that the CBC may feel it necessary virtually to eliminate its regional broadcasting merely exacerbates this problem. To make the point from a slightly different angle, as Marc Raboy does in *Missed Opportunities*, "official" Canadian culture as defined in broadcasting policy has become an instrument of the state; it serves the needs of the state, not the diverse needs of Canada's many peoples. The *public* interest has been submerged by the drive to sustain the *national* interest.[48]

Finally, Canada is totally misguided to adopt policies that close it off from the rest of the world in any way. We live in a global village, and should take advantage of the ability of our media to offer us a window on the world. Ideas and information are too important to be stopped at borders. Protection just encourages the development of inferior materials; our audiences must be given the chance to see the best quality cultural products available in the world and our producers the opportunity and incentive to seek global markets. This is of the highest importance in an age of globalization symbolized by the opening up of trade in goods and services everywhere in the world;

Canada will only be damaged in the long run by insisting on inward-looking protective measures that invite retaliation.

Rebuttal by Negative Side:

Far from harming Canada's national interests, American culture in fact helps bind Canadians together. It gives us myths, heroes, and guides for living that Canadians from coast to coast can share. Most particularly, we are united by the model of the affluent society in which we can all participate.[49] In a very profound sense, then, American culture is also Canadian culture. It has been the basis of the national unity we have maintained to date — a popular national unity, not one dictated from Toronto or Ottawa. Indeed, American culture is one of the great common factors between English and French Canadians; both groups would rather consume American culture than each other's.

Clear proof that American culture is not damaging to the Canadian identity is the fact that Canada still exists, although it has been flooded by Americanized mass media for at least the past one hundred years. Many strands, both material and spiritual, hold this country together; *People* and "Who Wants to Be a Millionaire" cannot destroy it. As Richard Collins put it, the assumption that political sovereignty depends on cultural sovereignty is not only mistaken but inappropriate to the present circumstances. Culture is becoming transnational (global), appealing across national boundaries horizontally; Canada demonstrates to the world the possibilities of this more integrated, non-national, future.[50] Moreover, Canadians are quite capable of intelligent selectivity. In fact, our access to American cultural products probably makes us less rather than more receptive to the American way of life. We have a unique view of both the best and worst of our neighbour; we can choose to adopt and adapt the best and discard the rest. We can be and are critical; we know who we are and what we want.

In 1985 the federal government commissioned a private poll on public attitudes to foreign ownership in the cultural industries. Although they were well aware of its extent, only 37 per cent of those polled considered foreign content a serious threat to Canada's national culture. The report given to the Department of Communication by the pollster Decima Research concluded: "Many Canadians feel comfortable enough about their own identities to believe exposure to American culture will not undermine their own sense of Canadian identity."[51] More recently, a COMPAS poll taken for the Friends of

Canadian Broadcasting showed that the percentage of Canadians who believe that our sense of cultural identity is strong or very strong rose — actually *rose* — from 29 to 38 per cent between 1993 and 1999, while those who believed it to be weak or very weak fell from 32 to 26 per cent.[52]

Rebuttal by Affirmative Side:

The large Canadian consumption of American mass media culture is not a natural phenomenon at all. It is the product of a complete misconception — that culture is a commodity. But culture is not a product like any other, it is a social good. It should not be sold in the marketplace by profit-seeking enterprises but should be developed as a public and national service. To some extent, in fact, American involvement in our cultural sector has not been "natural" at all but quite a deliberate part of U.S. government policy. For example, for many years the United States kept its postal rates for international second-class mail very low in order to stimulate the export of newspapers and magazines displaying the American world view.[53] It also allowed cartels like the Motion Picture Export Association of America to act in collusive ways contrary to domestic American law in the world market. The American government also fought long and hard to prevent Canada in the 1920s from getting a larger share of the radio spectrum allocation for North America, as it has more recently fought against developing countries at the international level. These are only a few instances of deliberate rather than natural factors lying behind the large consumption of American cultural products not only in Canada but worldwide. It is no accident that the United States has become the "world's only information superpower"; as a former official in the U.S. Department of Commerce expressed his vision in the late 1990s: "For the United States a central objective of an Information Age foreign policy must be to win the battle of the world's information flows, dominating the airwaves as Great Britain once ruled the seas."[54]

That Canadians watch so much American TV, buy so many American magazines and so on is a product principally of the availability of these products. This is not a choice made by the viewer or reader, it is the profit-driven choice of the owner, distributor or advertiser. The low Canadian demand for some specific indigenous products such as English-language TV drama and films is not "natural" at all, but the result of the fact that for many years Canadians were not offered anything else; they became conditioned to like

American products because they lacked any alternative. "Tastes in viewing and listening are not innate qualities of the human species but are acquired by exposure and are shaped by what is available."[55]

Canadians have also indicated in many polls that they support government intervention in the cultural sector. A 1996 Angus Reid survey, for example, found that 78 per cent of Canadians supported government measures protecting Canada's cultural industries and even more — 84 per cent — favoured the exemption of cultural industries from free trade agreements. The 1999 COMPAS/Friends of Canadian Broadcasting poll determined that the vast majority felt that the CBC's funding should either be maintained at present levels or increased.[56]

We need government intervention in the mass media sector in order to make Canadian culture available to Canadians. No one wants to exclude foreign voices entirely, only to make more room for Canadian ones. Government intervention does not prevent choice, it enhances choice. It gives Canadians the freedom to choose Canadian that they would otherwise lack. Freedom of the press is indeed important, but it is not an end in itself. The press is only one part of the whole community, and does not have the right to injure that community in the name of a principle that often is simply a cover for profit-making.

We will leave it to each reader to decide which side has the best of the debate. Canadians clearly hold diverse views on these matters. Canada may or may not be a model for the future globalization of culture, but it is certainly a case study showing that issues of culture and nationality are complex sources of contention among different groups within society. Governments have therefore been subject over the years to pressures both for and against protection of Canadian cultural expression on the mass media. Before we turn to examine some of the results in terms of policy, one more complicating factor must be discussed: technological change.

Technology and the Mass Media

Reconciliation of the tensions between economic and cultural priorities in the Canadian mass media is made even more difficult by the context of rapidly changing communications technologies. No sooner are business or policy decisions taken, it seems, than they must be reformulated to take into account new technological possibilities. One is reminded of the *New Yorker* cartoon showing a middle-aged man in a pin-striped suit having his tea leaves read. "You will never catch up with the new technology," the fortune teller confidently predicts.[1]

According to many writers, both experts and popularizers, we have now entered the "Information Age," a post-industrial era in which the production and exchange of knowledge and information is the driving force behind economic growth. Sophisticated communications systems are the vehicles for this ever-increasing data flow; each corporation's — and each nation's — prosperity in the future will depend on its ability to utilize the latest telecommunications equipment to control information exchanges in its own interest. The following is a fairly early expression of the theme:

> The explosion of telecommunications in the second half of the twentieth century may be compared to the transition that humans made thousands of years ago from hunting to agriculture, or, more recently, from an agricultural society to an industrial society. The transition of industrial societies, via the limbo of "post-industrial society," into fully-fledged information societies — as we witness now — makes telecommunications the hallmark and defining characteristic of our society. It is a measure of a society's wealth or poverty, and a major factor in a society's capacity for change.[2]

That statement was written in the 1980s, before an even more significant aspect of the new world of communication was apparent. The digital revolution, embodied in the rapid spread of computer usage, the Internet (including the World Wide Web) and the digitalization of both wired and wireless telecommunications networks has expanded the possibilities for the communication of information a thousandfold since. The new technology is of enormous relevance to the mass media, of course, for they have served for so many years as major information carriers. To what extent will their communications functions be altered by the creation of new delivery systems and increased demand for new forms of content — the so-called new media? Will the increasing capacity for international communication flows stifle Canadian cultural production or will it expand its possibilities? The mass media and the new media are increasingly intertwined as central issues confronting Canadian policy makers.

The Implications of Technology

In order to assess these new technologies, their impact on the mass media, and most importantly, how Canadians might respond to them, it is necessary to understand not only their technical capabilities but also the broader question of how technology inter-relates with cultural, economic and political elements in our society. Four major positions on technology and its social role may be distinguished in the literature, in various combinations. Two main polarities are identifiable, between determinists and non-determinists, and between optimists and pessimists.[3] Technology is usually defined in this literature to include not only tools and machines but also the productive and thought processes involved in their use.

Determinists essentially see technology as an autonomous and inexorable force, over which society has little or no control. Once unleashed, it shapes the economy, the culture, perhaps even human nature. The inherent characteristics of the technology (particularly its drive for productivity and efficiency) determine its evolution and demand its utilization. Debate about possible social consequences is almost irrelevant; simply because it exists, we must use it — such is the "technological imperative." Joyce Nelson has quoted J. Robert Oppenheimer: "It is my judgement in these things that when you see something that is technically sweet, you go ahead and do it and you argue about what to do about it only after you have had your technical success."[4] The technology to which Oppenheimer referred, of course, was the atomic bomb.

Non-determinists, while agreeing that technology is extremely powerful, nevertheless see human beings as even more potent. We can make the choices to use or not use technological inventions, to shape them according to our own priorities, for good or ill. Technology, then, possesses no magic powers; it is only one of many facets of society. Proponents of this view often particularly emphasize that the utilization of new technology depends upon decisions made by the major economic interest groups and therefore that technological innovations normally support rather than challenge the status quo.

The second important polarity lies along an optimistic/pessimistic axis. From one viewpoint, technology is the engine of progress. Without the machine, and without the rational techniques and procedures developed around the machine, we would still be living in a primitive, uncomfortable world. Technology has freed the western industrial nations from hunger and want, and if properly introduced, can do the same for the Non-Western countries. Technology is essentially emancipatory; it has extended man's abilities and the potential for democratic self-governance. By improving transportation and communication it is also helping to end narrow parochial nationalism.

The alternative argument, of course, is that technology has been the instrument of the obliteration of all that is most important in human society; it has isolated, alienated, homogenized, dehumanized and destroyed. French thinker Jacques Ellul, for example, and Canadian George Grant both deplore technology's transformative power. Not only has it altered how we do things, but also how we think about them. As a result, we are virtually unable to step outside the kind of rationalist, bureaucratic thinking engendered by technology in order to criticize it.

The Communications Theory of Harold Innis

The general dynamics of the debate about technology have been reproduced in the discussion about the particular type of technology of interest to us here, communications technology. One of the most influential thinkers in this area was a Canadian, Harold Adams Innis. The ideas of the Toronto school, as Innis, his "disciple" Marshall McLuhan and their followers are generally termed, have spread far beyond Canadian borders and have had considerable influence on modern communications theory.

Harold Innis, born in rural Ontario in 1894, was by training and profession an economic historian; for many years until his death in

1952, he was the head of the Department of Political Economy at the University of Toronto. Innis's early work centred on the concept of "staple trades" as the key to explaining the history of colonial economies like Canada's. His first important book, *The Fur Trade in Canada*, published in 1930, set the pattern by explaining how the pursuit of the fur staple shaped not only the economy of New France but also its institutions, society and politics. Moreover, the steady movement west and north along the waterways in search of furs formed the basis for the eventual east-west political structure of Canada that stretched across the northern half of the continent. While previously Canada had been conceptualized as a rather anomalous political formation imposed upon more "natural" north-south geographic lines, by linking economic, transportation and political factors Innis showed that Canada emerged "not in spite of geography but because of it."[5]

This did not mean, however, that Innis concluded that Canada possessed an inherent geographical unity.[6] The nation had been built in an era when the primary staple goods were exported along water and rail routes across the Atlantic to Europe. But in the early twentieth century new staples developed, particularly minerals and pulp and paper, whose main market lay to the south in the United States. Canada had become marginal to a different empire. Innis viewed this trend as a fundamental challenge to Canada's national integration; the effect of the new staples would be, he feared, divisive and centrifugal.

In endeavouring to understand how economies based on staple exploitation develop, Innis devoted much attention to technologies of transportation and communication. He was interested not only in how goods and people moved, but also in how information, particularly about prices, was transmitted. This interest intensified and combined with a preliminary study of the pulp and paper staple into a significant new project upon which Innis embarked in 1940: an exploration of communications in world history.

Although he never published a fully developed cohesive statement of his ideas about communications, the main outline is contained in two major essay collections, *Empire and Communications* (1950) and *The Bias of Communication* (1951). Essentially, Innis argued that any civilization may be understood as a function of its principal medium of communication. He treated communication technologies in much the same way as he had economic staples: as the prime determinants of institutional, cultural and social formation. Innis assumed that technology serves as an extension of man; communications technology is particularly powerful because it extends thought and consciousness. "The communications media — are literally extensions of the mind."[7]

It was not so much the content of the communications media that interested Innis as their form (or, as McLuhan put it, "the medium is the message"). He argued that some media tended to persist over time (for example parchment, clay and stone), while others (like papyrus or paper) dominated large territories, or space. The particular "bias of communication" of a society influenced both its institutions and its culture. In a time-biased civilization history, traditions, community, moral order, ceremony, religion and hierarchical institutions were valued. A space-biased civilization emphasized growth, expansion, empire, present-mindedness, science, materialism and secular authority.

The modern world, clearly, had a pronounced space bias. The invention of printing in Europe in the mid-fifteenth century, enabling the mass production of written matter, had not only foreshadowed mass production as an industrial system but had resulted in the rise of nationalism and the extension of political bureaucracies. By the twentieth century newspapers and magazines had become vast monopolies of communication, whereby imperial states like the U.S.A. controlled far-flung empires. Although Innis wrote little about the electronic media, the hints he dropped suggested that he viewed radio as an extension of print, enabling the further expansion of print-based empires.

For Innis, the principal dialectic was between the centre and the margin. He believed the history of civilization to be characterized by successive patterns of centralization and decentralization; only when the two forces were in relative balance was stability maintained. The key to historical change lay in conflict over control of communications systems as competing social groups fought for monopolies of knowledge. Innis thus approached the ideology of nationalism from a functional standpoint. Nationalism could be harmful if it led to excessive centralization and monopolization of power; on the other hand it could be beneficial on the margin as a counterforce against empire.

In this perception lay the roots of Innis's Canadian nationalism. He wrote pointedly and specifically about the alarming extent to which Canada had become a communications dependency of the United States, exporting vast quantities of pulp and paper to New

York and Chicago, only to buy it back in the form of newspapers filled with the American world view. While initially hopeful that identifying the "limits" imposed by economic and technological factors would help Canadians also find the "margin" in which they could manoeuvre, in his last years he became almost totally pessimistic. "All we can do in Canada is protest against *Time, Reader's Digest* and the like. We dislike them intensely but can do nothing about it," he wrote to a friend in 1949.[8]

Innis's concept of communications technology as the central determinant of social change throughout the history of western civilization reinforced and encouraged the study of mass communications theory. One of the major reasons for its continuing impact is his linkage of technological determinism to economic, political and cultural imperialism. His arguments about the spread of homogenizing secular empires via the print media seem even more apt today as we debate the potential effects of electronic messages transmitted via satellite and the Internet to all corners of the world.

More specifically, Innis's contribution has remained central to the Canadian debate. His perception that Canada by the middle of the twentieth century was subordinate to the modern monopoly of knowledge centred in the United States is repeatedly re-echoed in Canadian cultural nationalist thought. His thesis has provided the theoretical groundwork for contemplation of one of the central paradoxes of Canadian history: how technology in general and communications technology in particular have acted as a double-edged sword that simultaneously facilitates the promotion of national unity and serves as the highway on which the culture of another nation rides into our homes.[9] George Grant in *Lament for a Nation* pointed to the irony of a country like Canada, as a nation the product of the modern age, trying to establish itself as an independent entity by embracing technological change. "Nationalism can only be asserted successfully by an identification with technological advance," he wrote, "but technological advance entails the disappearance of those indigenous elements that give substance to nationalism."[10]

In the past thirty years new communications technologies like coaxial and fibre-optic cables, broadcasting satellites and computers and the Internet have come into widespread use. Major readjustments in the cultural sector have been occurring for a decade, and more are to be expected. Innis would have argued that we need to comprehend clearly the historical and economic context in which these new technologies have developed in order to understand the limitations they impose and therefore our margin for manoeuvre. The question of the moment is: "To what extent can Canadians guide and control these new technologies for the maximum benefit of all? Can we find the balance?"

The New Communications Technologies

At the beginning of this chapter it was suggested that the mass media are greatly affected by the so-called "information revolution" and the development of new technologies in the telecommunications sector. The fact of fundamental importance is that previously reasonably distinct boundaries between telecommunications, computers and cultural industries have become blurred in the past couple of decades and will continue to get even more fuzzy. This phenomenon of convergence has two major consequences: increased competitiveness among the different services and increased internationalization. In order to discuss these changes reasonably clearly, we will endeavour here to keep the focus on the technological developments most directly involving the mass media: coaxial and fibre optic cables, satellites, and digitalization. Because technology involves not only tools but their utilization, we must also consider the growing competition to provide cultural and informational services among telecommunications companies, cable companies, traditional broadcasters, film studios, website designers and others. The focus will be on the electronic media, especially television, because that is where the major impact lies, but it should not be forgotten that the introduction of the computer has transformed the internal workings of the newspaper and magazine businesses, as has the use of satellites to transmit copy over long distances.

The first widespread innovation after the introduction of television in Canada in 1952 was colour. As with the arrival of TV itself, a lag behind the United States occurred. CBC and CTV did not begin broadcasting in colour until late 1966. By 1977, five years later than in the United States, 70 per cent of Canadian families had traded up to a colour set. Although stimulating receiver sales and adding to the costs of program production, the introduction of colour TV did not entail a major restructuring of the industry. Probably the same will be true of the introduction of high-definition (digitalized) television (HDTV), which is anticipated by 2007 in Canada. Manufacturing companies will be enriched, but there will be no fundamental alteration in economic or social relations.

The other early innovation, once it caught on, had a much more profound effect. Coaxial cables were first used in Canada in the early 1950s on a small scale to provide television service to communities distant from broadcasting stations. Television signals reliably carry only about 100 km. To overcome this, enterprising companies constructed wirelines or large antennas that picked up the signals of over-the-air broadcasters and then sent them into subscribers' homes by connecting cables. The cable companies earned their revenue mainly from monthly fees; in the early days most of these companies were American-owned, but a Canadian-ownership requirement was introduced in 1968. Cable subsequently also proved useful in enhancing local service in large cities as interference from high-rise buildings became troublesome. It also provided better reception in southern Canada of colour TV and of nearby American signals. Most important, after a regulatory decision in the early 1970s to allow carriage of American signals to cable company antennas by microwave, Canadians in communities far from the border finally achieved "equality" with their compatriots in southern Quebec, Ontario and British Columbia who had had access to American TV since the late 1940s. In 1968 about 13 per cent of Canadian homes had cable, by 1973 that number had leapt to 33 per cent and by 1982 to 60 per cent, making us one of the most-cabled countries in the world. Today more than 75 per cent of Canadian homes subscribe to cable. Cable companies have regularly upgraded their lines to offer not only the standard twelve channels that old TV sets could receive but more and more additional ones.

While initially the signals distributed by cable were for the most part those of over-the-air broadcasters, the technology also opened up the possibility of a proliferation of new kinds of "program-packaging" (or "audience-assembling") companies not tied down by the capital investment involved in owning transmitters and other hardware. This type of company soon developed into pay-TV and specialty channels available only by paying a subscription fee. Pay-TV was first introduced by Home Box Office in the United States in 1976 and started out much stronger there than in Canada, primarily because Canadians already had more choice available (both the Canadian and American networks) on basic cable service. A pay-TV company is essentially a schedule organizer, purchasing material from producers and then selling the package to cable companies that have customers willing to pay extra above the basic cable-subscription rate for the special service. The signals are scrambled; only those

who pay the surcharge can receive them. Feature films were originally the mainstay of pay-TV but other specialized channels featuring sports, news and music videos and partially financed by
advertising as well as cable fees, provide the bulk of programming
now.

The introduction of pay-TV into Canada was delayed by the
CRTC until 1982 for fear that it would simply become the vehicle
for more and more American programming. When the regulatory
body finally did authorize pay-TV it required the successful applicants to commit a certain portion of their profits to the development
of Canadian programs. Far too many competing services were licensed, however; after the shakeout only the movie channels First
Choice: SuperChannel (now TMN, The Movie Network) and Super
Écran, and the specialty services The Sports Network (TSN) and
MuchMusic survived. Later the Life Channel and two third-language
services, Tele-latino and Chinavision, were also licensed. In 1987,
in considering a second major round of applicants for specialty channels, the CRTC moved TSN and MuchMusic (and their French-language equivalents RDS and MusiquePlus) onto "basic cable" (no
supplementary fee beyond the regular subscription cost) and licensed
a total of four more English and three more French basic services,
among them CBC's news and information channel, Newsworld, and
religious and family channels. In the 1990s many more specialty
channels have been licensed, available in various forms as extended
services beyond "basic cable." Some examples include Bravo!, Discovery Channel, Women's Television Network (WTN), Showcase,
History Television, The Aboriginal People's Television Network and
Réseau de l'information (RDI) — the French Newsworld. Several of
these — such as CTV's Newsnet — are owned by the old networks,
who have moved into this area in self-defence. American specialty
services that do not compete directly with Canadian ones are also
widely available when packaged with a certain number of Canadian
channels.

The arrival of cable distribution technology had a substantial impact on over-the-air broadcasters. Whereas previously in most communities except those close to the border the CBC and CTV split the
audience between them, after the introduction of cable they everywhere faced the competition, at a minimum, of the three major
American networks and PBS ("3+1" in the jargon), as well as of other
Canadian stations and networks, and later the American Fox network. For example, in 1984, in English-speaking Canadian homes

without cable, 36.9 per cent watched CTV, 31.3 per cent CBC, and 12.2 per cent other English Canadian stations, while about 19 per cent watched American channels. In those homes *with* cable, 22.4 per cent watched CTV, 18.9 per cent CBC, and 18.4 per cent other English Canadian stations, while the proportion watching American channels doubled to 38 per cent. On the French-language side, noncable households watched TVA 42 per cent of the time, Radio-Canada 38.9 per cent and English-language stations about 15 per cent; those with cable watched 32.5 per cent TVA, 31.8 per cent Radio-Canada and over 30 per cent English-language stations (including almost 14 per cent U.S.)[11] While French Quebec is less cabled than the Canadian average, those figures are alarming to Québécois fighting to preserve the French language.

Related to the expansion of channel availability is yet another new technology, fibre optics, which the telephone and telecommunications companies have begun developing seriously. The term describes a thin glass filament over which voice and data signals are moved by light wave (lasers). These glass threads have many advantages over conventional copper wire and coaxial cables for the transmission of data. Most important, they have enormous, and continually expanding, carrying capacity. Telephone and cable companies are working constantly to upgrade their trunk and local lines to increase carrying capacity in this way. Equally significant is the growing use of digital compression technology, which can accommodate more channels in the same bandwidth. In the late 1990s and early 2000 a number of new channels accessible only digitally were approved by the CRTC (for example Star! and ROBTv), and more will soon be onstream.

By the time specialty channels were finally authorized in Canada they had to meet another already-established alternative, the videocassette recorder or VCR. Introduced into North America in 1975, VCRs only became widely popular in the early 1980s when prices became reasonable. Eighty-five per cent of Canadian households now have video machines. VCRs have widened consumer viewing choice in a different way. Much of their use is for watching movies or other material (e.g. exercise programs) on tapes that may be purchased or, more commonly, rented from stores that have sprung up all over (some of them owned, in a typical hedging of bets, by cable companies like Rogers and Vidéotron). While the reproduction quality may leave something to be desired in comparison with attending the cinema, the price and convenience are strong selling points (not to mention the lesser censorship). Issues of visual quality have been addressed as well with the more recent spread of digital video machines and disks. While access to movies on video has had some negative effect on traditional exhibition venues like cinemas, film producers and distributors still make money from them, even if on a reduced and delayed basis, and some films are produced for video release only. VCRs have also changed viewing habits by enabling the recording of television shows to be watched at a more convenient hour. Some evidence suggests that the majority of programs time-shifted by Canadians are American movies, prime-time series and daytime soaps; in other words, the practice allows for the watching of even more American programming.[12] In one of the typical "Next Big Thing" scenarios that appear in our newspapers almost daily (and it is important to note how much the media hype the transformations occurring in their own world), it seems that we will soon all be buying Personal Video Recorders or PVRs, which will digitize TV programs, store them on a hard drive, and enable all sorts of personalized scheduling, pausing and instant replays.[13]

Another new technology, the communications satellite, has brought even more television stations into Canadian homes. The first communications satellite experiment was conducted by NASA in 1958. In 1972, with the launching of Anik A-1, Canada became the first country in the world with its own commercial domestic communications satellite in geostationary orbit (36,000 km above the equator in a fixed position relative to a point on the earth). While Telesat Canada, which owns and operates Canada's satellites, was originally owned 51 per cent by the government and 49 per cent by the telephone companies, the latter effectively controlled it even before the government sold its shares to them in the early 1990s. Telesat developed several more Anik series, of which three remain operational. Nimiq, launched in 1999, is Canada's first Direct Broadcast Satellite; the Anik F series of even larger and more versatile satellites will be launched in the coming years. The Canadian government was strongly motivated to get involved in satellites early because of the obvious advantages for a country subject to "the tyranny of distance and population dispersion"[14] as well as the opportunity to develop a technology with good potential in export markets.

The great advantage of satellites for telecommunications is their insensitivity to distance — that is, the cost of sending a message is not dependent on the distance it travels. Satellites are now routinely used for overseas telephone service, electronic mail, the transmission of computerized data and other business information, and for search and rescue operations. Several North American newspapers, among them the Toronto *Globe and Mail*, also use satellites to send computerized copy to printing plants in different locations across the country. The great advantage of satellites for broadcasting use is that satellite transmissions may be simultaneously received over very wide areas; the "footprint" or coverage area of Anik E-2, for example, comprises all of Canada and most of the United States.

The earlier less powerful satellites required large and relatively costly earth-station receivers. The first significant broadcasting use of these satellites was therefore what is called satellite-to-cable. A broadcast signal can be transmitted by satellite to the cable company's "head-end" receiver much more cheaply and efficiently than the traditional wire or microwave link. The CBC began using Anik A-1 this way very shortly after its launch to distribute both television and radio programming to northern communities, for example. Satellite transmission is now used routinely by broadcasters for coast-to-coast live broadcasts; satellites also carry Canada's national specialty and pay-TV services. Their digital compression technology offers the potential for almost constant expansion of channel capacity.

Signals from more powerful recent satellites (direct broadcasting satellites — DBS) can be received by much smaller and less expensive dishes. The multiplication of these dishes in remote areas unserved by cable companies, primarily picking up American signals, led the CRTC in 1981 to authorize the licensing of several Canadian satellite services. Among the regional services put into operation were two owned and operated by native organizations. The major player, however, was a company called Cancom (51 per cent owned by WIC Western International Communications of Vancouver), which was given a licence to provide a satellite-sent package of four Canadian TV stations and six radio stations to subscribers in remote and underserved communities across the country. In 1983, after pleading that it was having difficulty attracting subscribers, Cancom was permitted to add the American 3+1 networks. Thus, as Matthew Fraser points out in his recent book about the "digital frontier," the satellites put into place to ensure Canadian control of a new communications technology quickly proved to be "remarkably efficient importers of foreign cultural signals."[15]

The greater challenge to Canadian regulators, however, was the fact that Canadians with dish receivers could also easily get American programming direct from American satellites. Despite a ban on this practice, and the eventual creation in the late 1990s of two Canadian companies to provide direct broadcast satellite service everywhere in the country (ExpressVu and StarChoice), a considerable "grey market" of Canadians subscribing to American satellite services via U.S. post-office boxes still exists.

One of the attractions of satellite service for consumers is the availability of pay-per-view television, a system whereby the subscriber (to either cable or satellite) can purchase for a fixed sum, on a discretionary basis, the right to see a movie, sports event, concert or other specific program without having to stir from his or her couch. An experimental pay-per-view service as a cable option commenced in Saskatchewan in 1990, and Viewer's Choice Canada began permanent service in eastern Canada in 1991. While pay-per-view via cable has not been particularly successful so far in Canada, it seems likely that its usage will expand as satellite service does.

In general, the effect of the development of coaxial cables, satellite-to-cable and direct broadcasting satellites, VCRs and pay-TV has been an increase in consumer choice. Up to fifty television channels are now available in most Canadian homes, and there is little doubt that this number will increase markedly in the future. The implications of expanded specialty cable, satellite and pay-per-view service for other systems of distribution are enormous. As audiences fragment by moving to these specialized services, advertisers will follow them. Already 35 per cent of Canadians' television viewing is of specialty channels; it is predicted that a similar proportion of advertising money will be targeted there within ten years. The conventional networks and advertisers will see their falling audiences plummet even further and traditional modes of government regulation will become less and less viable.

The so-called "new media" are the culmination (for the time being!) of the technological and economic developments just described and of their convergence with the computer. In essence, the key to the new media is the digital revolution — the discovery of how to code massive amounts of information with a simple on/off electronic message, within or between computers or for wired or wireless transmission. A number of consequences have ensued: first the adoption of the computer as the principal means of gathering, storing and sharing information and the subsequent development of the Internet (initially by the Pentagon in a deliberately decentralized architecture) and its expansion to multimedia uses with the invention of the World Wide Web concept. It is impossible to speak definitively about the future social functions of the Internet, although we can be certain that they will be enormous. Matthew Fraser sums it up nicely:

> Will it serve as a telephone — or "videophone"? Will it be a television? A home movie theatre? An information-gathering device? A global e-commerce shopping mall? An international e-mail network? An instrument of education and enlightenment? A new form of publishing with computer-downloaded books? A global conduit for pornography and hate literature? All of the above? At present, no one knows for sure. Yet hundreds of millions of dollars are being invested on the basis of these various scenarios ... If anything is certain, it's that the Law of Unintended Consequences will likely impose its quirky logic on the Web just as it has on so many other new technologies.[16]

A second consequence has been the push towards digital carriage in the conventional media — on satellite transponders, on cables that bring telephones and television into our homes, on radio transmitters. The great advantage of digital transmission, wired or wireless, is that an immense amount of information can be sent in a very short time. This opens up the possibility for more channels for conventional media (the "500-channel universe") and thus throws the whole traditional concept of "spectrum scarcity" into disarray. A third consequence of the digital revolution, then, is that there are many more possibilities not only for businesses involved in the carriage of media but also for those who develop content. Moreover, content in digital format is more transferable — the most obvious example being the already-developed capacity to listen to a distant radio station or watch a movie on one's computer screen. The fourth consequence, therefore, and the sum of all the others, is that these developments have impelled the media industry toward both technological and corporate convergence. Installing the equipment necessary for the vastly expanded transmission possibilities is costly, and companies interested in such a venture — as all must be to survive — must take on heavy debts to do so. To protect their investments, they want to guarantee that they will be able to attract customers — that is, consumers for the new information and entertainment services that they will be able to offer. To decrease their risks, companies that originally provided carriage only — for example telephone companies like Bell Canada — are buying up not only satellite services but content providers like television networks. The traditional separation between media delivery systems (carriage) and programming (content) is vanishing. Broadcasters compete with cable companies, cable operators with telephone companies that are themselves no longer monopolies, and satellites with terrestrial communications. As technologies converge, old institutional and economic relations are in rapid evolution toward convergence as well.

One useful way of understanding the fundamentals behind the mad old/new media scramble in the early 21ˢᵗ century is to focus on the consumer in the home. There are two main ways that wired media come into our homes — via telephone lines and television cables. The cable companies have the advantage that their coaxial — and especially fibre-optic — connections have a broad bandwidth that can carry more information more quickly than conventional telephone lines. The advantage of the telephone companies is that their switching systems are designed for interactive interconnections. So far most of us get our Internet link through the telephone lines; the supply of high-speed service on cables with higher capacity is lagging behind the demand, but will undoubtedly improve in the near future. As to wireless connections into the home, for a variety of reasons, including regulatory stalling, this service is still very undeveloped. Despite some growth of satellite services and local wireless systems using antennas and dishes, for the foreseeable future the vast majority of Canadian telephones, televisions and computers will be served by coaxial and fibre-optic cables of one sort or another. Once in the home, these wide bandwidth channels can download information to our TV sets, our PVRs, and our computers — so the functions of these devices become almost interchangeable as well. We can indeed anticipate a "connected future."[17]

Because both the mechanisms of signal carriage and those of reception are rapidly being upgraded to digital capacity, the mechanisms of content production are inevitably affected. Increased capacity leads to increased demand for content. Traditional content producers like broadcasters and especially film production companies will have many new opportunities — the tremendous growth of Canadian film and television production in the 1990s is an example of what the future promises. Those with "libraries" of content from the past will find they can sell their material to the highest bidder; this is one of the main factors that has fuelled the interest in mergers between distribution companies of various kinds and Hollywood studios. The demand for new media content based on interactivity will also multiply — website design, information and entertainment software, games and so on, will remain growth industries. It is not clear how all of this will fall out in the next decade. There is a long way to go before the promises of universal rapid-access Internet (the Information Superhighway) linked to the 500 (or is it 1,500?) channel universe come to fruition. We should heed the caution in the words of one sour computer-industry executive: "The Internet and television are quite different media and they ain't going to merge."[18] As already described in Chapter 4, however, the major cable, computer, film and broadcasting companies have been consolidating their holdings and staking their claims to control the digital information multimedia future. The chances that this sector will end up more concentrated and more profitable for the handful of winners are very high indeed. Future developments promise to be interesting; it seems unlikely, however, that they will deviate much from the patterns of consolidation in the hands of the few that have been developing in the media business for the past century.

Although the dizzying whirl of change may make it seem that all this is inevitable, this is not the case. The introduction of these new services is being driven by private enterprise seeking profits and by government regulators who blow hot and cold but in general have encouraged the process. This leads to a couple of areas of particular concern. A number of writers have pointed out that because the introduction of these new services is profit-driven, and because much of the new technology involves costly and risky investments, the new communications products will inevitably be targeted toward higher-income consumers. In the old television network days, anyone could be part of mainstream North America for the cost of a TV set. TV thus spread extraordinarily rapidly in the 1950s. Now, basic cable costs about $25 a month, and extra services add considerably more. Direct satellite reception is still more costly. Digital television and radio will require the purchase of new sets all round. All of this suggests that the new technology will be fairly slow to penetrate; many of the forecasts one sees in the newspapers or company prospectuses are wildly optimistic. Predictions of 63 per cent Internet households in 2005 (31 per cent high speed), of digital cable/satellite in 10 per cent of households in 2000 and 25 per cent by 2005,

Personal Video Recorders in 60 per cent of homes by 2010 and so on, not only highlight how far all of this has yet to go, but more importantly that it will be a long time before even a majority of Canadians participate in this technological revolution.[19] Moreover, and very importantly, the high cost of the new technologies may be the basis for the widening of the gap — the "digital divide" — between rich and poor in our society based on access to entertainment and information. Even in early 2000, for example, less than half of Canadian homes have a computer, and only half again have Internet access. Insofar as the proliferation of these new technologies weakens the traditional and less expensive ones, the poor will lose, and the promise of communications to *increase* social linkages will have failed.

This leads of course to the second area of concern, the cultural. First of all, the new distribution technologies have opened Canada up to American programming in unprecedented quantities and in forms beyond governmental control. Cable companies have been importing American signals for more than two decades, although they are susceptible to some regulation. Direct broadcasting satellites, on the other hand, can bring American stations directly into Canadian homes in a manner almost completely beyond regulation. VCRs are also impossible to regulate. And most importantly, of course, the Internet "mocks political boundaries."[20] Not only is it incapable of regulation, but the CRTC has already announced that it has no intention of even trying. Secondly, as distribution capabilities have expanded in the past decade, program production has not kept pace. Opportunities for independent production companies have multiplied in the past few years; in Canada, Telefilm's Broadcast Program Development Fund has helped encourage that trend. Co-productions both national and international are multiplying. But the revenues from the many competing new services are not yet sufficient to sponsor enough production to fill all the hours. Programming dollars are spread very thinly. One alternative is the re-run, and many of the specialty channels fill much of their time with recycled programming. The other alternative, only too tempting in Canada, is to continue and even increase the purchase of those inexpensive and popular American shows that have been the mainstay of our television schedules since the 1950s. A whole new generation is currently watching "Lassie" and "Buffy the Vampire Slayer" on channels like YTV and Showcase. By acquiring sophisticated cable, satellite, VCR and other technologies, by in effect allocating our resources to equipment before programming, Canada has expanded an infrastructure that not only allows but encourages the entrance of even more foreign content with a competitive advantage in our marketplace.

To a considerable extent, Canada has acquired this new communications technology without considering its cultural impact in advance. As innovation followed innovation, businessmen looked for market opportunities at home and abroad, consumers looked for greater choices in in-home entertainment, and governments looked for ways to keep both groups happy. One-time minister of communications David McDonald remarked that our communications policy has been characterized by "Technopia Canadensis," "a condition of intense focus on hardware and new technologies causing an inability to see long range effects." He went on:

> The Canadian record in communications technology has been consistently one of world leadership in the research, development, and engineering of new delivery modes for television — and just as consistently, of failure to adequately consider and plan for what those systems would carry ... *Canadian* initiatives — *Canadian* hardware — *foreign* content — it is a recurring saga, but we seem unwilling to act on the lessons of our own experience....
>
> Characteristic of our relationship to technology is a lack of planning until its introduction is a *fait accompli*. It seems, too, that benefits are mostly enjoyed at the private level (be they corporate profits or a new gadget for the home), while negative effects are left to the public arena to redress.[21]

Awed by the possibilities of the communications revolution, few have considered — until too late — its cultural impact. One basic assumption has governed: that Canada must adopt the latest technology or risk losing control of its communications destiny.

This takes us back to where this chapter began, to Harold Innis. Not only does it suggest an underlying technological determinism but it recalls Innis's concerns about imperialism and dependency. Decisions taken in the United States inevitably impinge on us directly, as a result either of economic links (such as information exchange within multinational companies), of media links (satellite signals flowing freely across the border), or of social and cultural links (the demand of Canadian audiences for "equal" access to American popular culture). Canadian policy makers are caught on

the horns of a dilemma. Even when they recognize potentially negative cultural consequences, they are unable to say "no" to technology.
The authors of the Caplan-Sauvageau Report stated the problem this
way:

> On the one hand, policy makers in broadcasting may want to
> put the emphasis on program content. Especially they may not
> want to see money diverted from programming to equipment,
> since Canada is at a disadvantage in meeting costs of program
> production by comparison with the United States. On the other
> hand, this country cannot afford to lag far behind the United
> States in adopting new technology; otherwise it would abandon
> to the United States the provision of services based on the new
> technology.[22]

The conclusion we reach, then, is that it is not the technology *per se*
that has driven this story. Always, decisions made by businessmen
and choices made (within the range of options available) by consumers have influenced the development of different technologies. Both
have functioned — especially in the field of communications —
within a framework of government regulation. It is to that topic we
must finally turn. Is it still possible in the age of the digital revolution
for the Canadian government to guide our mass media toward goals
that are in the country's self-interest? And can we agree on where
that interest lies?

The Government and the Mass Media

The mass media have been assigned two main political tasks in western countries: the implantation of the values of good citizenship and the dissemination of the news, opinion and debate necessary to the proper functioning of a democratic government. These two goals, however, are not necessarily always congruent. In Canada, for example, governments have looked to the mass media to help create and express a sense of unity and identity to weld together a vast and disparate nation. But their concurrent concern that the media be free of government patronage so they can act as vehicles of open and informed discussion and criticism has led to private-ownership patterns that have resulted in very high levels of concentration in the hands of a few and have fostered a very large foreign presence in our media.

Another problem is that no government can act in media affairs without political implications. While generally any government intervention in the economy or society can have or be seen to have partisan motives, this issue is particularly delicate vis-à-vis the mass media because of their central importance in modern political life.

As we have seen, the Canadian newspaper business from the early nineteenth century on was an intensely partisan activity. While direct links between political parties and media outlets have pretty much passed from the scene, the importance of the media to politics has not declined but rather grown in this century, especially since the arrival of television. As our society and country have become larger, more complex and less community-oriented, the media have played a greater role in conveying political information, positions and values to the voters. "For the majority of citizens in mass societies such as Canada, the principal continuing connection to leaders and institutions is provided by the words, sounds and images circulating in the mass media."[1]

The debate about the significance of mass-mediated politics parallels the more general debate outlined previously. Liberal-pluralist, Marxist and other paradigms may all be applied to the political "effects" of the media, depending upon one's point of view. Of particular interest in this case have been two issues: the effect of television's "jolts-per-minute" demands, and the relationship of journalists to political news. As to the first, it is evident that in the last two decades politics has become more and more a matter of personalities, of candidates' television "presence," and of their ability to compress complex issues into visually interesting, brief "sound bites." Underlying themes and long-term ramifications are ignored in favour of quick, superficial and conflict-oriented snapshots.[2] On the second issue, the academic consensus seems to be that politicians have become masters of manipulating the press by controlling access, using their own pollsters and advertising agencies and so on. In response, at least part of the press has turned to a kind of "attack" journalism which has made it vulnerable to accusations of bias and to renewed efforts by the politicians' "spin doctors" to control all political discussion. Voters, in turn, have become disillusioned with the whole business.[3] Thus, while as a whole the media reinforce and legitimate the existing political system, they have also altered many of its characteristics.[4] Not only specific issues but the functioning of democracy itself have been marked by the massive impact of the mass media on the political process.

Canadian governments over the years have in fact introduced a number of measures that in various ways encourage, aid or protect segments of our cultural industries. A number of principles lie behind these policies; generally they strive simultaneously to encourage nation-building, individual liberty, equality, regionalism and efficiency.[5] The difficulty is not only that these interventions have often been motivated by political considerations, but that inherent contradictions among the various goals have resulted in cultural policies rooted in ambivalence. In this chapter we will examine the measures currently in place under five categories: ownership, subsidies, tax concessions, other legislation and regulation. Interwoven with this discussion will be some consideration of the policy challenges the government faces at this moment of transformation in the media industries. We will concentrate on the actions of the federal government, since most of the major initiatives have been taken at that level. In 1980 responsibility for most of the federal government's activities in the cultural sector was assigned to the Department of Communications (DOC). A major change occurred in 1993 when the DOC was dismantled and its job split between the Department of Industry (telecommunications policy) and the Department of Canadian Heritage (broadcasting, other media and the arts).

Ownership: The CBC and NFB

Currently, the federal government spends about $2.6 billion a year on culture, an amount that is in steady decline when inflation is taken into account. A good proportion of that money is spent on parks, museums, archives and other areas that do not concern us here. Almost half of it, however, is spent on broadcasting. Most of that goes to the publicly funded broadcaster, the CBC.

As we have already seen, the CBC was created in 1936 to provide a national broadcasting service that would cover the whole country and provide an alternative to American radio. In the early 1950s the CBC was given the responsibility of setting up the first television stations and network as well. Today the CBC operates not only French and English television networks but also two 24-hour specialty news channels, Newsworld and RDI, two French and two English radio networks, a radio and television service in the North, and it manages the international shortwave service Radio-Canada International. As of 1999, the CBC distributed its programming by satellite, cable, microwave and landlines to 95 CBC owned-and-operated radio and TV stations, over one thousand rebroadcasters, 27 private affiliated stations and almost 300 affiliated or community rebroadcasters. The CBC is Canada's major broadcaster, both in terms of budget and of program development. It is also the greatest factor distinguishing our broadcasting system from the American one.

The CBC currently operates under the authority of the 1991 Broadcasting Act. That act specifies that the CBC should provide "a wide range of programming that informs, enlightens and entertains," that this programming should be "predominantly and distinctively Canadian," should "be made available throughout Canada" and should "reflect Canada and its regions to national and regional audiences, while serving the special needs of the regions." It also calls for the CBC to provide service "of equivalent quality" in English and French, "including the particular needs and circumstances of English and French linguistic minorities," to "reflect the multicultural and multiracial nature of Canada" and to "contribute to shared national consciousness and identity." This is a much larger and more specific task than that assigned to the private broadcasters, who are asked "to an extent consistent with the financial and other resources available to them" to "contribute significantly to the creation and presentation of Canadian programming" and to "be responsive to the evolving demands of the public." All broadcasters, both public and private, also fall under the act's general rubrics that the Canadian broadcasting system "shall be effectively owned and controlled by Canadians," that they must "make maximum use, and in no case less than predominant use, of Canadian creative and other resources," and that they must produce "varied and comprehensive" programs of "high standard." Reinforcing the importance of the CBC to the system, the act also specifies that Canadian broadcasting constitutes a "single system" and that where conflicts arise between the CBC and other broadcasters, they are to be resolved "in the public interest," with the CBC's objectives taking precedence. Compared to the 1968 Broadcasting Act which it replaced, the 1991 act was significant for its softening of the CBC's old mandate to "contribute to the development of national unity" and its emphasis on regionalism and multiculturalism.

Given the great and complex responsibilities with which it is charged, it not surprising that the CBC has been subject to numerous criticisms over the years, which have tended to make successive governments cautious and sensitive about its role. The corporation's greatest vulnerability lies in its direct funding by Parliament. Although it is operated at arm's length by an independently constituted board of directors and management, the CBC's reliance on annual parliamentary allocations has tied its fate closely to political trends and budgetary exigencies. Every commission or committee that has examined the CBC has recommended that it be given longer-term grants to allow it greater independence and manoeuvrability but this step continues to be resisted by governments that want to keep the corporation under close supervision. The English-language CBC and French-language Radio-Canada operate as virtually separate entities. The Quebec nationalism evident at Radio-Canada since the Quiet Revolution has been a particularly sensitive issue in Ottawa.

The CBC has also been attacked frequently — both from within and without — for its large bureaucracy and top-heavy over-cautious management. Because traditionally most CBC programs have been produced in-house (although this is no longer so much the case), the organization employs a complex mixture of creative, technical and management personnel, a mixture that can at times be volatile. The

CBC is also highly unionized, which increases its costs and decreases its flexibility in comparison with the private broadcasting sector. In general, the CBC is subject to the same kinds of criticism directed at most crown corporations in these neo-conservative days, most particularly that it is less efficient and more wasteful than similar enterprises in the private sector.

In addition to this general criticism, most of the negative commentary focuses on CBC television, and especially English-language television (although a similar critique of Radio-Canada is developing as well). The radio network, which long ago dropped commercials and focussed on public-service and high culture programming for small audiences, is generally praised for doing things right; among CBC radio's biggest fans are the private broadcasters who are delighted not to have to face the corporation's commercial competition. As for the television networks, the CBC's programming has been faulted simultaneously for both élitism and pandering to the masses. On the one hand, many Canadians feel that it has over-emphasized serious and high-culture programming. While widely admired for the excellence of its news and public-affairs shows, the CBC's efforts in popular dramatic and entertainment programming have been notably less successful. Even Radio-Canada, with a much stronger tradition of providing popular indigenous dramas and variety programs, is by no means the recipient of universal praise. On the other hand, intellectual and cultural élites who look to the CBC to provide enriching fare distinguishable from that offered by other broadcasters have frequently condemned the CBC for buying popular American programming to attract audiences and advertisers, and for producing imitation-American programs when it does venture into its own prime-time drama. In this more "purist" view, the CBC should be a sort of PBS-North, concentrating on encouraging Canadian cultural production of the finest types and contenting itself with smaller audiences if necessary. To date, the CBC's management and the federal government have consistently held to the view that the CBC's mandate is to be a major, not a peripheral, player in the Canadian broadcasting game but their ability — or will — to continue to defend this position is currently in doubt as the CBC, like every other media institution, confronts the challenge of the tremendous changes of the new millennium.

The corporation has also been the object of frequent attacks from west, east and north for its centralist bias. While much money is expended on regional and local programming, most of those programs are for local consumption only. Regional stations and production were disproportionately targeted in the budget reductions made between 1981 and 1989, and were particularly hard-hit by cuts in 1990. Ten years later, much regional programming has disappeared, and the remaining portion — especially the supper-time newscasts — is in jeopardy. The majority of network programs come from the two main production centres in Toronto and Montreal, and the major decisions are made by central management in those two cities and in Ottawa. The corporation's decision in the early 1990s to spend hundreds of millions of dollars on a showpiece Broadcast Centre in Toronto has particularly disgusted many in other parts of Canada. One consequence of this tendency to centralization over the years has been the weakening of regional cultural expression; in the period when CBC radio was almost the only vehicle in Canada for English-language drama, for example, those who wished to be involved had no choice but to move to Toronto. In other regions of the country, the CBC is often seen as yet another federal agency reinforcing the Ontario-Quebec domination of the national agenda, and is heartily resented for it. While the CBC has never fully satisfied its mandate to enable Canadians to speak to one another from region to region or from culture to culture (and has been markedly unsuccessful in sponsoring French/English dialogue), whatever successes it had in the past are lamented today by those who foresee that financial exigency will result in even greater centralization in Toronto.

The Broadcasting Act gives the CBC great responsibilities, and virtually every observer has pointed out that no government has given the CBC the resources with which to accomplish this task. Although it has much higher technical costs due to the large area and scattered population it must serve, per capita the CBC receives less government funding than similar public broadcasters in most European countries. One product of the permanent shortage of money is the affiliate system in existence since the CBC was founded; the need to satisfy the different priorities of privately owned affiliates skews the corporation's decision-making. The 20 per cent of its budget derived from advertising revenue is important to the CBC for the same reason, and results in programming shaped to commercial priorities. At the same time, the CBC's competition for advertising dollars creates resentment among the private broadcasters who have no government subsidies to fall back upon.

In recent years the CBC has never had the popular or political support necessary for substantially increased federal funding; on the contrary it has been subject to consistent budget cutbacks. Between 1984 and 1991, the CBC's parliamentary allocation fell by 16 per cent in terms of purchasing power and by 20 per cent as a proportion of total federal expenditures. Between 1993 and 1998 it dropped by $300 million to a now-stabilized level of about $750 million a year. Three thousand employees have been released since 1995, leaving about 7,000 in late 1999, with more cuts anticipated. According to former CBC manager Peter Herrndorf, this sort of attrition has had extremely negative effects on the CBC: "Instead of a national voice, it's a national whisper."[6]

The federal government spends considerably more on the CBC than on any other cultural endeavour. It is by far the government's major commitment in the battle to wrest the mass media out of foreign hands. Nevertheless, it does not spend enough to enable the CBC to fulfil the duties it has been assigned. The future of the CBC is currently being carefully considered by its management. That less than 10 per cent of the English-speaking population watches CBC television, and even less in major centres like Toronto (the figure is about 20 per cent for Francophones), has given even some of those who have traditionally supported the CBC pause. Maybe the time has come, they suggest, to admit that the CBC's main appeal is to minority tastes that cannot be supported by the market, and that it should find for itself a niche role as a group of specialty services. Many neo-conservatives make this argument because they assume the government's willingness to fund the corporation as a niche broadcaster would be minimal; some CBC supporters also prefer this option because of their distress with the commercialization of the TV network caused by the desperate battle with the private broadcasters for audiences and advertisers. The argument is quite convincingly made that while once the CBC had to be "all things to all people" because it was the only network, or one of only two of three, now this is no longer the case. Compromises such as commercialism, popular American programs, and wall-to-wall hockey are no longer necessary or desirable. Indeed, why should the government fund a public broadcaster that looks only too much like the private ones? As this is being written, among the possibilities that would move the CBC in the direction of more focused "narrowcasting" being debated — within and outside the CBC — are the separation of production, transmitting and scheduling into separate units (as the BBC has done), the abandonment of the corporation's terrestrial transmitters in favour of cable and satellite distribution, reduction or deletion of the regional supper-hour news broadcasts, the removal of advertising from the TV network, and complete decentralization to the regions accompanied by the sale of the Broadcast Centre. Generally, the common theme is that the CBC should emphasize its *difference* from the private system by focusing exclusively on Canadian content and on the programming it excels at, such as documentaries, current affairs and news. On the other hand, as the Friends of Canadian Broadcasting lobby group points out regularly, the adoption of almost any of these suggestions would have the cumulative effect of alienating most of the CBC's remaining audience, completely undermining its political support in Ottawa and elsewhere, and above all, of clearly violating the responsibilities assigned to the corporation by the 1991 Broadcasting Act.[7] A CBC that deliberately served only a small minority would soon lose its political credibility — and even more of its funding. It is perhaps not surprising that the CBC itself has so far been unable to face up to such a major transformation of its role — this is a matter that goes far beyond the institution itself to involve both government and the larger society.

The CBC has always played an anomalous role in Canadian broadcasting. While charged with the cultural responsibility of protecting the national and public interest, it has from the beginning been only one part of an otherwise commercially oriented system, within which it must compete for audiences, money and credibility. In the effort to serve all Canadians equally, the corporation has tended to allocate its insufficient funds to distribution over programming, which even further weakened its cultural role. More significant than the lack of money from the government, however, has been the lack of commitment. From the initial decision taken in the 1930s not to restrict the private-radio sector, to the more recent decisions encouraging the fragmentation of the television market, government policies have been as often detrimental to the CBC's ability to serve Canadians as supportive of it. As Marc Raboy argues, the CBC has consequently become a model of "administrative broadcasting," which serves not the public interest but that of the state, the government of the day, and itself.[8] Nowhere is the fundamental ambivalence of Canadian cultural policy more evident.

The other major media institution owned by the federal government is the National Film Board. The Film Board, set up in 1939, has generally played a much less central role than the CBC despite its broad mandate to produce and distribute films "in the national interest" that will "interpret Canada to Canadians and other nations."

As already noted, while the Film Board has achieved widely admired successes in documentary and animated films, it has not been a major player in the feature-film business in Canada, either for theatrical or television release. Certainly distribution difficulties have been a factor in the former case, but it is not so clear why NFB films have not been more frequently used by Canadian network television, especially the CBC (in 1986–7, NFB films accounted for exactly twelve prime-time hours on the CBC network). The CBC has claimed it lacked available prime programming hours and that too many NFB films are of poor quality, are inappropriate for television, or are not sufficiently "balanced" to meet the CBC's special responsibilities in treating controversial subjects. Generally, the NFB has been traditionally more successful in gaining viewers for its French-language than its English-language endeavours, and a number of NFB-sponsored French-language feature films, including "Mon Oncle Antoine" and "Le Déclin de l'Empire Américain" have been very successful.

Recently, the NFB has been undergoing some important changes. In a thorough restructuring, permanent staff positions have been reduced so that more production money can be channelled to freelancers across the country. Seventy per cent of its work is now done on a freelance basis. No more feature films are being made, and the sound stage and film laboratory have been closed. Co-productions are also becoming the norm. In the 1990s the NFB had considerable success with co-productions; both "The Boys of St. Vincent" and "The Valour and the Horror" generated large television audiences and extensive debate. Amidst internal transitions and economic constraints, the NFB (with an annual parliamentary grant of around $55 million) is moving to a greater presence in the mass media. While theatrical distribution will almost certainly remain only a small part of the board's activities, the marketing of videocassettes is being actively pursued, as are new distribution possibilities through specialty TV. In 1994-5 about 75 per cent of the Film Board's TV distribution revenues came from provincial educational stations or specialty channels like Vision, Bravo! and Discovery. While this has meant an impressive growth in audience, the specialty channels pay little for these films, so the NFB's budget is not much enhanced. In the mid-nineties the NFB also began distributing some of its films to educational institutions through the Web in a project called CinéRoute. Most of those who view NFB films now do so not in the traditional schoolrooms and church basements, but in their own homes on TV or video.

The CBC and the NFB were both set up as federally funded media institutions in the 1930s out of a conviction that they were necessary to enable Canadians to speak to one another. The CBC was intended from the beginning to be a major part of the structure of a new industry; the NFB was conceived as somewhat more marginal to the mass-media market. Through the years they have had many ups and downs and have been the centre of considerable contention about their role, purpose and even existence, and that kind of questioning is now more intense than ever in the context of a decade of government downsizing and major reconfiguration of the media environment. Numerous critics of the CBC and NFB may be found on both sides of the cultural-nationalist fence. All of this, of course, has had considerable negative political fall-out. It is thus not surprising that, when Canadian governments have found it necessary to aid needy sectors of the cultural industries, they have often preferred more indirect measures to ownership.

Subsidies

The federal government has subsidized the newspaper and magazine industries for over a century by granting postal rates for second class mail well below (by as much as two-thirds) the actual cost of carriage. More recently, direct-subsidy programs have been introduced to encourage television and film production.

The federal government began subsidizing Canadian newspapers and magazines by means of reduced postal rates in the late nineteenth century. Publishers lobbied for this benefit on the political and cultural grounds that it was important for Canadians to be well informed about their country and its government. Administrations intent on nation-building, and on "helping out" important political allies, obliged. The cost of this program was carried for many years by the Post Office, and it was often cited as a major factor in Post Office deficits. In 1985–6 postal subsidies for newspapers and magazines cost the Post Office — and the Canadian taxpayer — $225.1 million; at the time this was "by far the largest subsidy program offered to any cultural industry in this country."[9]

Various arguments may be made both for and against the second-class rate policy. Some have criticized it on the grounds that most of the content of newspapers and magazines is now advertising, which means that our tax dollars are going to subsidize advertisers. Similarly, it has been argued that the large conglomerates that now own so many of our print media hardly need the taxpayers' aid. Moreover, the policy also subsidized American magazines trucked into Canada to be mailed here. On the other hand, postal distribution is not a major factor for newspapers any longer. Magazines have been the principal beneficiaries of this provision; "little" magazines catering to specialized groups have been the most dependent upon the program for survival. Postal subsidies have also been viewed as one of the more defensible forms of aid to cultural industries in that they are indirect, involving no interference with content. The Special Senate Committee on the Mass Media (the Davey committee) in 1970 examined the whole subject closely, and concluded that subsidization should continue because it genuinely served readers' needs.[10]

Nevertheless, in the 1990 budget, the federal government announced it would be winding down the postal subsidies over the next four years, and replacing them with a grant program administered by the Department of Communications (now the Department of Canadian Heritage) totalling about 50 per cent of the previous expenditure ($110 million). Ottawa's argument was that the old program was too all-inclusive, and that the new plan would better target worthwhile Canadian publications while raising rates for such material as trade and foreign publications. The large cutback in expenditure, combined with the heavily criticized decision to apply the GST to books, magazines and newspapers, as well as the advertising income lost during the economic downturn, had very negative effects on the magazine publishing industry in the early 1990s. Although the situation improved somewhat by the end of the decade, the reduction in the postal subsidy helped foster a trend toward more controlled-circulation magazines.

The second major area in which subsidies have been offered is much more recent, and also much more direct. After many years of concern about the scarcity of movies featuring Canadian stories and Canadian stars, and after the failure of various other programs, in 1968 the federal government set up the Canadian Film Development Corporation, now called Telefilm Canada. The purpose of the agency is to foster and promote the development of feature film and independent TV production in Canada under two programs, the Feature Film Fund and the Broadcast Program Development Fund (introduced in 1983 and targeted toward drama, children's, documentary and variety programming). In both instances, the intention is to encourage private-sector projects by aiding the development, production and marketing of film products. Some of the cost of the Broad-cast Fund is covered by a tax charged to all Canadian cable subscribers (hidden in their cable bills). There is also a special program to help finance dubbing to encourage English-French exchange and a special distribution and publicity fund. A further program was added in 1996, when what is now called the Canadian Television Fund was set up with a $200 million allocation. About half of this money, the Equity Investment fund, is administered by Telefilm as well. The investment money allocated under Telefilm's various programs is intended to complement, not replace, private funding. Strict definitions of "Canadian" are imposed by this program, as well as strict regulations requiring advance distribution contracts; funded TV programs must have a previous commitment that they will be shown in prime time, for example.

Telefilm Canada has generally been a popular and successful cultural agency. Over three decades it has provided about $1.6 billion in support for 1,600 television programs and almost 700 feature films, among other things. The Broadcast Fund particularly has been very successful in encouraging production of good dramatic serials for both public and private television. About half of the Broadcast Fund's expenditure traditionally has gone to productions for the CBC; the fund is thus an indirect means of subsidizing the CBC. But its extensive financing of programs shown on private stations ($81 million between 1986 and 1990) is one indication of the extent to which private broadcasting in Canada is also a state-subsidized venture. An increasing proportion of Telefilm funding goes to programming for the specialty channels — not surprising given the fact that some of them have very high Canadian-content ratios. An increasing amount is going into foreign co-productions as well. Not everything is rosy, however. While there have been some big successes like "Jésus de Montréal" and "The Sweet Hereafter," few of the feature films financed by Telefilm have made money, in large part because of the traditional difficulties in getting Canadian films distributed in theatres. Overall Telefilm-assisted productions remain 60 per cent publicly financed — in other words, private investment from broadcasters, distributors and others still constitutes less than half of the financing of these productions. Nevertheless, Telefilm's aid has undoubtedly been important to the substantial growth of the Canadian film and TV production industries. In 1997 that industry had total revenues of over a billion dollars, profits of about $86 million, and about 20,000 workers. About a third of the sales revenues came from exports, especially of TV programs. A significant amount of American television and film production now occurs in Canada, as well — enough that various Hollywood interest groups have begun to complain. All in all, one can only agree with Tom McSorley's suggestion in *Take One* that perhaps the Canadian film industry has finally reached critical mass, and that much of the credit must be given to Telefilm Canada, "one of the most important, influential, impressive, infuriating, inscrutable and inspiring" of Canada's cultural institutions.[11]

Subsidy programs, even indirect ones, have political implications. While many economists believe that they are the best way to stimulate Canadian culture, because they can be targeted at specific goals and then assessed for efficacy, this does leave them vulnerable to partisan manipulation. Other interest groups may well question whether the government should be aiding private entrepreneurs who may be perfectly capable of getting along without help. Alternatively, doubts may be raised about whether enterprises that would fail in the competitive marketplace should be artificially propped up with taxpayers' money. Nevertheless, these two major subsidy programs exist because of the conviction of the Canadian government that the media they support — newspapers, magazines, film and television — make significant contributions to its goals for the nation. The original postal-subsidy program, however, primarily served economic rather than cultural interests. It favoured publications indiscriminately with little regard for their Canadian content or ownership, or their need. In that sense its replacement (despite reduced funding) is an improvement, although there will undoubtedly be room for debate over which publications are targeted for aid. The Telefilm subsidy, especially for broadcasting, being better-defined, is one of the most successful cultural programs currently in place. It too has been hit by cuts in recent federal budgets, however, and is under attack in some quarters for an increasingly commercial emphasis.

Tax Concessions

In addition to subsidies charged to the Department of Canadian Heritage, the federal government grants tax breaks to a number of cultural industries. In the sense that this is forgone revenue for the government ("tax expenditure") and reduces the producer's costs, these measures also act as subsidies to the media.

The newspaper and magazine industries traditionally benefitted in this instance by being exempted from the 11 per cent federal manufacturers' sales tax charged on both imported and domestically produced goods. This exemption cost the federal government an estimated $90 million a year before it was in effect cancelled by the decision not to exclude publications from the controversial replacement for the manufacturers' tax, the GST. In the magazine sector, as much as two-thirds of the benefit used to go to non-Canadian magazines; now Canadian and American magazines sold here are equally burdened.

The 1965 amendment to the Income Tax Act (Section 19) regarding deductibility of advertising in Canadian magazines and newspapers has also acted to subsidize publishers and broadcasters by means of a tax break. It will be recalled that this measure was introduced with the intention of encouraging advertisers to utilize Canadian media in order to strengthen their revenue base. Money spent on advertising in Canadian newspapers or magazines or on Canadian broadcasting stations is deductible from the advertiser's tax bill as a business expense. Necessary to the legislation, of course, was a definition of "Canadian," which proved the most controversial aspect of all. As a general consequence it has become financially unviable for a non-Canadian to own a Canadian newspaper, magazine or broadcasting station, regardless of any other existing laws regarding the nationality of media owners. (Since 1968 there have also been explicit rules requiring Canadian ownership of broadcasting outlets and cable companies.) These provisions have the effect of reducing the amount of competition faced by Canadian corporations in the cultural sector, which is also of benefit to them.

A possibly unintended consequence has occurred in the television field. Whereas bolstering the revenues of Canadian magazines results in more Canadian content, because most magazines import little of their editorial material, quite a different effect occurs on television. Cultural policy analyst Paul Audley, for example, argues that the tax breaks given Canadian television advertisers go mainly to support American programming, because most ad dollars are spent on the imported segment of the broadcasting schedule.[12] The benefit helps Canadian media owners; it does not directly address the question of Canadian media content. In that sense, it is an industrial policy, and only secondarily cultural.

Yet another tax exemption package illustrates even more effectively some of the flaws that can undermine the intentions behind such arrangements. In 1974 an amendment was introduced to the Income Tax Act to offer a 100 per cent Capital Cost Allowance (CCA) on investments in feature films meeting certain qualifications. The conditions included having a Canadian producer and having a number of other creative functions performed by Canadians. Later the program was extended to include television programs. The estimated forgone federal revenue in 1979 was $8.5 million. A remarkable increase in the amount invested in Canadian feature films occurred — from around $20 million in 1977 to $140 million in 1979. In order to recoup the investment, however, it became necessary to sell these films in foreign — read American — markets. The result was to encourage films not recognizably Canadian in any way; "Meatballs" remains the epitome of the genre. One critic wrote: "The 100 per cent Capital Cost Allowance stands as a monument to irresponsible policy making and comes as close to being a pure taxpayer 'rip-off' as one is ever likely to find."[13] Canadian cinema became "a strange land," another commented, "where sportswear manufacturers and government bureaucrats, periodontists and psychiatrists were gripped by a primitive and irresistible impulse to hurl money into production of excruciatingly empty movies."[14] Even the "Americanization" strategy was not enough to bring in satisfactory returns; the result was an abrupt plummeting in investor interest. In 1987 the CCA was reduced to 30 per cent, despite opposition from the film industry. Both Quebec and Ontario subsequently instituted measures to try to replace this tax shelter because of the importance of the film industry to their provincial economies. The abuses that developed under the old CCA seem to have led the federal government, however, to conclude that much more careful guidelines are essential if such a program is to serve its intended purpose. In now orienting its largesse toward direct funding via Telefilm, an agency with considerable discretionary authority as to whom and how it grants money, the government in effect has gained more control over film policy. Nevertheless, the total amount of money going into film financing was considerably reduced as a consequence of the cutting back of the CCA, and in the late 1990s the government again reversed itself. Two programs to give tax credits related to the production costs and wages paid by film and video production companies — whether Canadian or foreign owned — were created. The eligibility of foreign (American) companies is, needless to say, controversial. Exactly how much this "giveaway to Hollywood" has cost Canadian taxpayers is not known, but it is estimated to be in the range of $50 to $100 million per year.[15]

A major question remains: Will the greater reliance on direct funding through Telefilm make a difference to the quality or Canadianness of the films made? Despite all the programs over the years to encourage Canadian cultural industries, this is a question which has more often than not been ignored, or answered only by instinct and self-interest. The difficulties in addressing it are manifold, but one interesting preliminary attempt was made in the late 1980s by two scholars from Carleton University.[14] Keith Acheson and Christopher Maule assembled a panel of sixteen film experts to answer a questionnaire about a random sample of forty Canadian films funded by CCA and released between 1974 and 1987. One half had also received Telefilm funding — in other words they had also been subject to more targeted funding policies. (The investigators, incidentally, did not use a general population sample in the survey because they concluded few would have seen the films.) The questionnaire addressed such issues as whether the respondents had seen the film, whether they had enjoyed it, whether the story line was distinctively Canadian, whether it would be attractive to Canadian audiences, and so on. The conclusion was that Telefilm-funded films were discernibly more available, more enjoyable and more Canadian. While the study was a limited one, it did suggest that the government is moving in the right direction in focussing on Telefilm if its intention is indeed to encourage both culture and industry.

At the same time, potentially contrary policies are also in evidence. Telefilm's strong emphasis on private investment and the tax credit program's sole focus on jobs rather than content have been reinforced by the increasing trend toward film and television co-productions, itself fostered by the growing international demand for programs as channels proliferate. International co-productions offer the advantage that they often receive domestic subsidies in both countries and can fit within domestic-content quotas where they exist. A number of Canadian production companies such as Alliance Atlantis have had considerable success with co-productions in the last decade. The Canadian market is simply too small to support a substantial film industry; only by sales and financing abroad can quality films be produced. Once again, however, the question is raised: Do co-production agreements promote Canadian industry or culture? While creating jobs in the film sector, which is surely a good thing, the resultant films and TV programs, it has been argued, are often of an indistinguishable transnational character which does not in any way fulfil the goal of enabling Canadians to speak to one another about themselves. A quality review panel set up by the Friends of Canadian Broadcasting, for example, concluded that "the need to appeal to foreign markets had led ... to a great deal of programming that is bland, safe, lacking in irony and out of touch with Canada's current social reality."[17]

In general, the various tax exemptions designed to help the cultural industries have demonstrated as many disadvantages as benefits. Often, the measures adopted have been inefficient in targeting their intended products and producers. Thus the excise-tax exemption benefitted the publishers of the thousands of American magazines that pour across the border, the advertising expense deduction has helped television stations that feature American programming, and the Capital Cost Allowance encouraged the development of "a very good American film industry in Canada."[18] Policy development in the cultural area requires very careful analysis of consequences, particularly when the benefits are granted indirectly. The policy makers at DOC and subsequently Canadian Heritage have not always been successful in achieving their ostensible goals. Primarily, this has been the result of the contradictions inherent in those goals: while they wish to foster Canadian cultural and informational exchange, they hesitate to intervene directly in matters of media content. Stimulative measures are therefore only reluctantly introduced, and when they are, they are targeted toward the producers, not the product. In too many instances, the results are as contradictory as their conceptualization.

Other Legislation

In addition to programs subsidizing cultural industries or giving tax breaks to encourage them, the federal government involves itself in encouraging the Canadian media by certain other measures that do not demand any substantial expenditure.

An important example of such legislation is the copyright law. Copyright is an extraordinarily tangled subject that cannot possibly be fully covered here. It needs some attention, however, because copyright is integral to the cultural industries. Not only does it to some extent control the flow of information and entertainment, but it also links artistic with commercial motivations. Copyright is important because it encourages the production of Canadian creative works.

The law of copyright gives the exclusive right to make copies or give performances of an original work to the creator of that work or those to whom he or she has assigned (usually sold or licensed) that right. It serves the purpose of ensuring a monetary reward for the person who has created the work by preventing others from using it freely for a fixed period. The 1921 Canadian copyright law under which most of our cultural industries have developed, protected the production and reproduction of "works" in any "material form" as well as the "public performance" of such works. The difficulty of course is that the law was written before radio broadcasting began, much less television, cable TV, audio or video tapes, computer programs and data banks, photocopiers or communications satellites.

While some of the technicalities of protecting authors' rights on radio broadcasts were hammered out in the 1930s, little else in the act was altered to bring it into line with modern technology. Thus, for example, a local broadcaster paid into a copyright fund in order to get the exclusive right to broadcast a given program in his market area. But as the result of a 1954 court decision that simultaneous retransmission of signals is not equivalent to radiocommunication of a work or a public performance, cable operators in that same market area were able to pick up the transmission of a distant station and supply it to their customers without paying any copyright fees. Legal loopholes like this existed because it became impossible to use old definitions of "material form," "public performance," or even "a work" to describe new transmission devices and capabilities.[19] Much of the Canadian cable industry was in fact built upon this particular loophole; if it had been more costly to import distant signals, Canadian cable companies might well have developed other program formats.

Copyright has considerable international repercussions as well. It is important that Canadian creators be protected at least as well as creators in those countries with which we exchange cultural goods and services. Conversely, it is also important that the weaknesses in the Canadian legislation do not create resentments that might lead to retaliation from other nations. The CRTC began allowing cable companies to import signals from the American networks in 1971. No compensation was given to the American producers whose shows were picked up; this created considerable concern in the United States, especially after that country in 1976 revised its own copyright law to protect the ownership right in signals. Canada consequently promised as part of the Free Trade Agreement to ensure that Canadian cable companies would begin paying copyright fees to the American producers by 1990, and this provision is now in effect. Payments of about $50 million annually are involved; in some cases part of this cost has been passed on to subscribers, and the rest has been absorbed by the cable companies; in other cases, it has resulted in companies dropping certain services.

In the 1980s a great deal of time and energy went into the first major revision of the Copyright Act since 1921, mainly in the direction of bringing the legislation into line with the technological changes of the past sixty-odd years and, if possible, with future developments. In 1989 a new law was finally passed providing for the setting up of a Copyright Board to enable the collection of copyright payments for a much more up-to-date list of transmission media and to increase severely the penalties for those who copy a work illegally. As is so typical, however, no sooner did Canada bring its copyright laws into the twentieth century than the twenty-first began. The huge problem of copyright on the Internet, where pirating of music and TV shows has already spawned lawsuits, has delayed the development of the Net as a media distributor and will continue to do so until some means of compensating copyright holders for the use of their material is sorted out.

A second area in which the first Mulroney administration considered legislating is an example of another type of non-financial aid the federal government can provide to help a cultural industry. As has already been pointed out, one of the greatest difficulties faced by the Canadian feature-film industry has been the control of film distribution by American subsidiary firms that do not for the most part either distribute Canadian films or reinvest their profits in them. In February 1987 then Minister of Communications Flora MacDonald announced a new bill giving Canadian film distributors priority over American distributors in the import of independently produced foreign films into Canada. The intention was to help the Canadians, who were more likely to reinvest in Canadian films, prosper. One DOC report suggested that Canadian distributors would gain $25 million by these provisions, enough to finance twenty new Canadian films. The bill aroused a storm of opposition in the American film industry and among its allies in Congress, who feared a precedent might be set that would affect the world film market. Michael Wilson's Finance Department was so concerned that it successfully pressured to have the whole matter quietly dropped until after the Free Trade Agreement had been signed.[20]

Subsequently a somewhat weakened bill was reintroduced but its effect has been minimal. Canadian film distributors have been somewhat appeased by the direct cash infusion they now receive from Telefilm. A very similar act in effect in Quebec is also a watered-down version of what that province had originally intended; it gives Quebec distributors priority for non-English-language films.

One final area of legislation, already mentioned, needs to be addressed, although it is not directly concerned with the cultural industries — and indeed specifically excludes them. This, of course, is trade legislation — the Free Trade Agreement (FTA) which came into effect between Canada and the United States in 1989, NAFTA, which extended the FTA to include Mexico, and the World Trade Organization (WTO) agreement of 1994, which substantially expanded global free trade in goods and services. The pattern has been similar in all three cases. From the moment the Mulroney government announced its intention to negotiate the Canada-U.S. Free Trade Agreement, a large number of Canadian cultural producers began lobbying vociferously to ensure that culture not be on the bargaining table. Their passion was rooted in the cultural nationalist assumption that the agreement threatened the intertwined triad of economic self-determination, cultural sovereignty and national identity. Assurances were quickly given at all levels that cultural industries would be excluded, and indeed a clause explicitly stating this point is in the agreement. Nevertheless, the FTA does impinge on culture in several ways. For example, concern about its passage, as we have just seen, influenced the dropping of the film distribution bill. The requirement for cable companies to pay copyright on retransmission was also part of the agreement. Moreover, the FTA contains a clause specifying that the United States may take retaliatory measures in *any* industry equal to the losses caused by continued Canadian protectionism in cultural industries. As several commentators have pointed out, if nothing else this clause codifies the American assumption that culture is a commercial issue, as opposed to the Canadian insistence that it is precisely because culture is more than a business that it does not belong in such a deal.[21]

The United States has continued to press this position in international trade forums — not surprisingly, given that cultural products are its second-largest export. When NAFTA was signed in 1994, the cultural industries again remained off the table, although Mexico, with a culture somewhat protected from the American by language, was not as concerned about the issue as Canada was. By far the major challenge to traditional Canadian cultural protections, however, is the WTO, where the American position has been dominant. Premised on the ultimate goal of global free trade in goods, services and investments, the WTO's intent is eventually to remove protective practices of any type. In the cultural area specifically, so far the General Agreement on Trade in Services (GATS) has provisions that allow nations to opt out of its application to the audiovisual market; Canada and most European countries have done so. But it seems unlikely that exemptions of this type will continue to prevail over the long term. As one media scholar sympathetic to Canadian culture but not to some of the means currently used to protect it puts it:

> The movers and shakers of the Canadian cultural establishment will soon ... have to admit the obvious: culture is on the table. The idea that cultural products and services are exempt (or should be exempt) from bilateral or international agreements is no longer tenable.[22]

This comment was made by Ted Magder with respect to the most important WTO decision affecting Canadian culture taken so far, the ruling on split-run magazines. Briefly, as mentioned earlier, *Sports Illustrated* (owned by Time Warner) began publishing a "Canadian edition" containing a small amount of Canadian editorial content and many Canadian ads. It evaded customs regulations against shipping editorial material across the border for such a purpose by transmitting the copy electronically to a Canadian-based printing plant. Canada retaliated by refusing to allow Canadian advertisers in the new magazine the normal tax deduction for expenditures in "Canadian" magazines. The United States appealed to the WTO, which ruled against Canada in 1996. Canada's response, an attempt to make it illegal for Canadian advertisers to buy space in U.S. magazines aimed at Canada, evoked an American threat of "equivalent action" against such Canadian products as steel (Canadian Heritage Minister Sheila Copps comes from Hamilton, a steel town). Finally a deal was reached that allows, after a 3-year phase-in period, American magazines with no Canadian content to sell up to 18 per cent of their space to Canadian advertisers (on a tax-deductible basis); more Canadian ads are allowed if there is Canadian content. The predicted fall in advertising revenues for Canadian magazines will apparently be compensated by direct subsidies.

The split-run affair is significant for two reasons. First, it is a harbinger of the future for traditional kinds of cultural protectionism; they are not going to survive the international trend, which Canada supports, toward freer trade. Secondly, in moving to a direct-subsidy approach, the government is introducing a program that is better-targeted than the old advertising-deduction scheme, which mainly benefited affluent consumer magazines owned by corporate giants like Ted Rogers. As Magder concludes: "Surely Rogers does not need government money to keep *Macleans* afloat. Public money should be earmarked to subsidize editorial content, not advertising ..."[23] While Magder is undoubtedly right, and there is no doubt that various Canadian policies of cultural protectionism have subsidized private economic interests with little real interest in fostering the diversity of Canadian cultural life, it is worth noting that more conservative commentators, like the editorial board of the *Globe and Mail*, have a different reason for supporting direct subsidy programs like this one: they are fully visible and therefore easily phased out. Indeed the *Globe* advocates exactly that; it longs for the day when all subsidies are removed and we have a "fully-open North American market for magazines." Canadians who want Canadian content in that circumstance will prove it by paying for it, the *Globe* optimistically predicts.[24]

As previously mentioned, Canada is not the only country that wishes to see future global free trade arrangements provide some sort of cultural protectiveness and the government continues to work with others toward this goal. Nevertheless, the enormous pressure from the United States affects Canada by far the most. Moreover, some elements within this country are also lobbying for changes in ownership rules particularly, both because allowing greater foreign ownership of newspapers or broadcasting stations, for example, would increase their value, and because an open market in Canada would pressure the U.S. to eliminate its own ownership rules (the U.S. has no restrictions on newspaper ownership, but does restrict foreign involvement in broadcasting). Increasingly, in a global marketplace, the Canadian government is going to have to look to trade-offs like this if it wants to maintain other kinds of protection such as subsidies and content quotas and if it wants equal opportunities for Canadian cultural industries to expand abroad.

Regulation

The final, and in some ways most controversial, type of government intervention in the mass media is its assertion of regulatory power over broadcasting. A number of rationales for the regulation of broadcasting exist. Their common theme is that because of certain specific attributes, broadcasting is different from other cultural forms in ways that justify — even demand — government regulation. The most important of these differences results from two assumptions: that the airwaves are a public resource and that "spectrum scarcity" exists. The argument is as follows. While it is theoretically possible for anyone to express his or her viewpoint on any issue in print by starting up a press, the limited number of frequencies available for broadcasting stations means that only some members of society can have access to the electronic media. Some way of allocating the privilege of broadcasting must then be determined. The conclusion that it must be the government or a governmental agency follows fairly readily. The airwaves are public property; the right to use them must therefore be determined by the representatives of the people rather than by market forces. The need for coordination with other countries and with other users of the spectrum also suggests that governmental involvement is necessary. Those granted licences to use the airwaves, by this same reasoning, become public trustees. They cannot use their frequency in an irresponsible manner. Most particularly, they must not use it to present a single or narrow viewpoint; rather, the owner of a broadcasting station must guarantee the right of his listeners to be informed by diverse points of view. On balance, the right of the public to hear is stronger than the right of the broadcaster to freedom of expression.

These concepts of public resource and spectrum scarcity have been the principal arguments used in most countries to justify not only government allocation of frequency assignments, but intervention in general program content to fulfil goals such as "balance" and "fairness." Even in the United States, with the strong First Amendment guarantee of freedom of the press, regulation of radio and television content has been accepted by the courts under this sort of reasoning.

Recently, however, the notion of spectrum scarcity has come under considerable fire. The most important cause is technological change. The expansion of capacity by means of cable, satellites, digital compression and fibre optics, while not unlimited, is already substantial, and will be more so in the future. In this more competitive context, the scarcity argument becomes less convincing as an excuse for governmental intervention in program content particularly. When there are only four channels, it may be justifiable that each of them provide balanced programming; when there are one hundred, the balance can be derived from the whole range. (It may be pointed out parenthetically, however, that the real constraint on freedom of expression for all is an economic one which applies to both print and broadcasting: very few have the financial resources to establish either a newspaper or a broadcasting station these days.)

A more recent and probably more compelling justification for broadcast regulation may be labelled the "impact" theory. According to this argument, television has much greater influence on its audiences than do the print media because of its immediacy and pervasiveness. Because the majority of people receive most of their news and information from television, in a uniquely face-to-face form of communication, and in a home environment, the medium is so powerful that it cannot be left to develop without concern for its social consequences. The Canadian adaptation and extension of the argument suggests that because of the particular historical and geographical position of this country, special intervention is necessary in this most influential of media to protect national goals. Specifically, for example, Canadian content regulations are justifiable from this point of view. The Caplan-Sauvageau Report stated the point uncompromisingly: "The assignment of radio frequencies for broadcasting in Canada is an essential component of national sovereignty."[25]

Opponents of regulation, on the other hand, insist that proof of the greater impact of television than of the print media is remarkably scarce. As we have seen, despite hundreds of studies, the "effects" of television remain debatable. American cultural economist Bruce Owen argues indeed that perhaps the vast power and influence of television is due not to its unique nature but to the fact that regulation based on assumptions of spectrum scarcity has forced vast numbers of people to watch the same programs on the same few networks.[26]

Whatever the strength or weakness of the various rationalizations for governmental regulation of broadcasting in Canada, such regulation has existed from the earliest days of radio, and it is unlikely that it will cease. Under the Radio Broadcasting Act of 1932, the CRBC, predecessor to the CBC, was given both national broadcasting and regulatory responsibilities. The CBC remained the regulator until 1958, when an independent body, the Board of Broadcast Governors

(BBG), was set up. Under the 1968 Broadcasting Act a new agency, the Canadian Radio and Television Commission or CRTC was handed regulatory powers (the name was changed to Canadian Radio-television and Telecommunications Commission in 1976 when telecommunications was added to the CRTC's responsibilities). The 1968 Act charged the CRTC to "regulate and supervise all aspects of the Canadian broadcasting system," including the CBC, and this responsibility continues under the updated act of 1991 (and for the telecommunications side, under the Telecommunications Act of 1993). It has the power to issue, renew or revoke broadcasting licences, and to set conditions both for the whole system and for individual licensees. The CRTC, however, is not a totally independent regulatory body. The government appoints its members and authorizes its budget; as well the government can set aside or refer back certain decisions regarding licences. One significant change in the 1991 act is that it gives the cabinet the power to issue directives to the CRTC not only about specified issues but also "of general application on broad policy matters" with respect to both broadcasting and regulation.

Since its establishment, the CRTC has handed down hundreds of thousands of decisions. Especially since 1976, when it was given responsibility for regulating telecommunications as well as broadcasting, it has had far too much to do with insufficient resources; critics have suggested that since that date, in a period when broadcasting has been under enormous challenge due to the proliferation of distribution technologies, the CRTC has acted more as a passive referee than an active shaper of the system.[27] More recently, the CRTC has seen its role as a more "supervisory" than regulatory one. Here we will confine our examination of the CRTC to three of the areas in which its decisions have been most significant: Canadian content on television, cable TV and licensing.

Content rules for Canadian television stations were first introduced by the BBG in 1960. According to these rules, 55 per cent of all programs broadcast, averaged over a four-week period, were to be of Canadian origin. The definition of "Canadian" was flexible; it included credit for programs from the Commonwealth or French-speaking countries and "broadcasts of programs featuring special events outside Canada and of general interest to Canadians" — which included, it turned out, the World Series. Later amendments both loosened and tightened the original rules: for example the 55 per cent was reduced to 45 per cent in the summer to help stations out over months when local production was low and the averaging period was changed to a quarter-year, but a quota of 40 per cent Canadian content in prime time was introduced to prevent stations from hiving off all the Canadian programs into the least-watched hours. Without going into detail about the various alterations in these rules over the years, we may summarize by specifying how they stand today. Current regulations require 60 per cent Canadian content, averaged on a yearly basis, from all stations. The CBC is also required to broadcast 60 per cent Canadian content in prime time (defined as 6 P.M. to midnight) while private broadcasters have a 50 per cent quota for prime time.

A number of problems exist with these regulations. First of all, they have gaping loopholes. The provision for yearly averaging allows stations to jam Canadian content into the summer months when viewing is least. The definition of prime time is overly generous; by allowing private stations to include their 6 P.M. and 11 P.M. newscasts as prime time Canadian content, it permits them to offer as little as 25 per cent Canadian material in the most popular and lucrative 7 to 11 P.M. slot. One study showed, for example, that in a fourteen-week period in 1988–9, CTV had only 30 per cent Canadian content in "peak" prime time, but compensated with 79 per cent in the "fringe" hours of 6 to 7 and 11 to 12.[28] While the CBC, which exists to a large extent outside the marketplace, has never had any problems with these regulations, the private broadcasting industry has often resisted and manipulated them because they cut into profits. As might be expected, the suggested minimums have become maximums. Harry Boyle remarked when he was chairman of the CRTC in 1977: "There is not a regulation that has ever been passed that someone cannot get around if they want to."[29]

An even greater — and less easily soluble — difficulty with the Canadian content rules is the fact that they regulate only quantity, not quality. Nowhere in the regulations is there more than the most general injunction that the Canadian programs produced should be of high quality and a varied nature. Because dramatic programming is very expensive, private stations rarely use it to fill the quota unless the CRTC specifically demands it; news, sports, and cheap game and quiz shows are much preferred. There has been no incentive to take any other route. This reality creates a real dilemma for the CRTC, for much as it believes it has the right to regulate content for nation-building purposes, it is reluctant to do so in more than the most general way. Specifying quality or even program categories treads dangerously close to interference in freedom of the press.

So, for example, the CRTC's definition of a "Canadian" program for the purposes of its regulations is a purely technical one, based on the nationality of those involved in its production. Yet a program produced following these guidelines need not necessarily have any identifiably Canadian references or characteristics at all. Independent producers are being encouraged from all sides these days to look to foreign markets for the salvation of the Canadian film and television industries, but productions aimed at foreign markets are particularly susceptible to fulfilling the letter but not the spirit of the Canadian content rules.

In addition to its reluctance to interfere in broadcasters' freedom to say what they please, the CRTC is also hamstrung by its belief that it must remain responsive to the economic needs of the television industry. Overly stringent rules reducing advertising income to the point where a station goes bankrupt is not considered a service to the Canadian public. That the CRTC has been sensitive to this fact does not necessarily mean that it has been "captured" by private interests, it simply means that the commission realizes that the television industry serves simultaneously economic and cultural goals. Nevertheless, the Davey committee's comments on the situation bear repeating: "We wish media owners, as an industry, would think again about the policy of maximizing profits by skimping on the quality of the product. The maximizing is their business. The skimping is everybody's business."[30]

Some changes in these traditional policies have been evident in the last decade. Since the late 1980s the commission has been imposing specific requirements as to expenditure on Canadian programs and numbers of evening hours devoted to Canadian drama on the private network, CTV, although to a considerably lesser extent on Global because until very recently it did not have national coverage and so claimed it was not a "network." While Canadian drama has become somewhat more available in the last five years, in part owing to these regulations and also because of Telefilm subsidies, nevertheless the general conclusion must remain that despite thirty years of trying, the CRTC's Canadian content rules have not worked. In the fall of 1998, for example, out of 28 hours of central prime time (7-11 P.M.) per week, Global averaged 2.5 hours of Canadian programming and CTV 6 hours. While some of the shows presented (like "Due South") were recognizably Canadian, others (for example

"The Psi Factor") were Canadian in name only. Meanwhile, the CBC filled 26.5 of 28 prime-time hours with Canadian content.[31] The principal reason Canadian content rules have not worked, and this remains true whatever conditions of licence are imposed, is because they do not solve the fundamental problem: that it is not in the economic interest of private broadcasters to produce Canadian drama programming.

Notwithstanding the CRTC's initiatives, Canadian content rules are even less likely to be effective in the future. Technological change is already providing consumers with more and more unregulated television choices, such as VCRs and complete foreign signals via satellite. As expanded choice places a greater competitive burden on private broadcasters they will seek even more ways to avoid having to use the profits they derive from American shows to cross-subsidize Canadian production.

The regulation of cable companies has confronted the CRTC with equally difficult, and somewhat related, dilemmas. As mentioned above, a 1954 court decision confirmed that it was legal for Canadian companies to continue the practice, which had already begun several years earlier, of erecting large antennas to pick up the signals of distant stations and then retransmit them via cables to paying customers. Until 1968, these companies operated without any but technical regulation. With the 1968 Broadcasting Act, however, they were brought under the jurisdiction of the CRTC on the grounds that they were "broadcasting receiving undertakings."

From the time it took charge, the CRTC was preoccupied with the threat cable penetration posed to the existing over-the-air broadcasters. Indeed, it may be argued that the CRTC was particularly worried about cable and solicitous of the profitability of the over-the-air broadcasters specifically because of the Canadian content burden it imposed on the latter.

As one result, the CRTC did not until 1971 permit cable companies to import American signals to distant communities via microwave connection. When it finally, under strong consumer and industry pressure, yielded in this respect, it introduced a number of policies to protect the interests of local over-the-air broadcasters. For example, cable companies were required to give priority to CBC and other Canadian local and educational stations.

Today, in addition to the rule giving priority to Canadian signals, there exist two main protectionist devices: the simultaneous substitution (simulcasting) rule and Bill C-58, both introduced in the mid

1970s. The former rule requires large cable operators, on request, to replace a foreign signal with a local one if the same program is being shown simultaneously. By this means the audience, and therefore the advertising revenue, of the local broadcaster is enhanced. The (presumably) unanticipated effect, however, has been to encourage Canadian broadcasters to air American programs in the same prime time slots as the American networks, that is, to adjust their schedules to foreign priorities. One outraged Canadian observer concluded: "The prime-time schedules of most Canadian television stations are programmed not in Toronto, not in Montreal, not in Vancouver, nor anywhere else in Canada. The decisions are made in Los Angeles by executives of CBS, NBC, ABC, and Fox. The history of Canadian television has been an inglorious saga of colonial dependency."[32]

Bill C-58, the 1976 legislation amending Section 19 of the Income Tax Act, was discussed earlier with respect to the magazine industry. Its provision that ads placed on American border broadcasting stations lose their tax deductibility caused great consternation in the U.S., and remains an irritant to this day. Again, the intent is to funnel Canadian advertisers' money to Canadian stations.

As the copyright ruling indicated, cable is a difficult industry to define. In some senses, it is a cultural industry in that what is carried by the coaxial or fibre optic cable is a number of broadcast signals containing the usual mix of news, information, entertainment and so on. A small amount of programming is also generated by the cable companies themselves on required "community" channels. Primarily, however, cable companies operate as carriers. Due to the high cost of installations, these companies almost invariably are granted territorial monopolies. As such, they may be likened to telephone companies or other utilities, except that telephone lines carry the messages of everyone willing to pay the cost, while cables carry only a limited number of selected messages.

Generally, the CRTC's cable policy has been faulted on two grounds. First, for years the commission allowed cable companies to expand in Canada on the basis of cost-free American programming, thereby fragmenting the market, hurting Canadian broadcasters, and decreasing the total amount of Canadian programming on our screens. Its attempts to protect Canadian broadcasters were purely economic in nature; while fairly successful in protecting their revenues, they did not address the overall diminution of Canadian content. Second, the CRTC's assumption that cable is a "hybrid," half broadcaster and half utility, was used to liberate these highly profitable companies from the most stringent regulations normally applied to both broadcasters and utilities. Thus cable operators were free of requirements as to Canadian content, balance and so on, yet simultaneously, unlike the telephone companies also under the CRTC's jurisdiction, they were free of monitoring for quality and reliability of service, and were not required to extend their service to lightly populated unprofitable areas.

Although both the CRTC and the DOC were originally reluctant to stimulate cable television, in the 1980s cable became their technology of choice. In a 1983 statement "Towards a New National Broadcasting Policy," then Minister of Communications Francis Fox announced that cable development would henceforth receive priority because it is "the most cost-effective means of significantly expanding the viewing choice of most Canadians, while at the same time ensuring that the broadcasting system remains identifiably Canadian."[33] The CRTC's bias in favour of cable has been confirmed by many subsequent actions detailed in Matthew Fraser's recent book, *Free-for-All*. Among them were the lengthy delay in granting licenses for cable's main competitor, satellite TV, and the willingness to allow the cable companies to be financially involved in owning satellite-TV companies. The CRTC also backed away from its traditional demand for separation of carriage and content in the late 1980s when it began to allow cable companies to own specialty channels. There are many more examples, but they are well summarized in Fraser's concluding comment regarding the CRTC's willingness, time and time again, to allow the cable operators to increase their charges: "Cable subscribers were not the CRTC's clients; the cable industry was."[34] What has made cable so attractive to the CRTC has been the fact that unlike some of the newer technologies like satellites and the Web, it is capable of regulation. As such, it can be used as an instrument, a gatekeeper; in return it legitimizes the role and existence of the CRTC — and of the Canadian state.[35] It is not surprising that the state's regulatory bodies would privilege media carriers they can still exert some control over; it is essential to recognize, however, that once again this policy is one in which signal delivery takes precedence over programming.

Like subsidies and tax breaks, regulatory policies often have unintended consequences. Those who write about regulation frequently point out that despite (or sometimes because of) the intentions of the governments that set up regulatory agencies, before long such bodies become "captives" of the very industrial groups they were created to control. Precisely that accusation has been made against the CRTC. Licensing practices provide the best example. Over the years, the CRTC has had the power to issue many licences for new radio and television stations. In these situations, the commission holds a hearing at which the various competitors for the licence present evidence as to their financial and programming plans; based on that information one of them is then selected to receive the licence. Normally, the promises made are grandiloquent; more often than one would like, they are not kept. The main penalty for performance failure available to the CRTC is revocation of the licence. It is a very harsh penalty given the heavy capital investment made and has therefore almost never been used. The 1991 Broadcasting Act did introduce for the first time a bit more leeway in this respect; negligent broadcasters may now be fined for minor transgressions insufficient to warrant licence suspension.

When licence-renewal time comes, the CRTC does not hold competitive hearings. The licence-holder is almost invariably given the go-ahead regardless of the quality of his service (although sometimes for a reduced term) and his competitors, who perhaps presented more realistic plans at the initial hearing, remain out in the cold. Similarly, when a licensee wishes to sell his company, it is CRTC practice to consider only the applicant proposed by the current licence-holder. The vast majority of such transfers are approved.[36] The CRTC has tended to look benignly as well upon concentration in the broadcasting industry and media cross-ownership on the grounds that large investors will more likely survive. The 1998 decision to allow multiple ownership of private radio stations in the same market is a case in point; it was justified on the grounds that the radio industry was in difficulty (although that has been disputed). It was also a fairly typical trade-off, however, because it was accompanied by an increase in Canadian music content requirements from 30 to 35 per cent.

There is little doubt why the CRTC acts so generously toward its licensees. Regulation involves quid pro quos. In exchange for the controls it imposes upon private businesses, a regulatory body must grant some benefits. The most important limitation the CRTC imposes on private broadcasters is the reduction in their profits resulting from the Canadian content requirement; the most important benefit it distributes to them is the right to hold a broadcasting licence. By the licence-granting practices as just described, as well as by other policies like the simultaneous substitution on cable rule and advertising deductibility and foreign ownership laws, the government and the CRTC in fact protect broadcast licence-holders from the exigencies of the marketplace. The very existence of the CRTC thus grants to broadcasters a considerable privilege not available in many other endeavours. Despite all their protests against specific policies they dislike, neither Canadian broadcasters nor cable operators can be heard calling for the dismantling of the CRTC.

> Whether in the protection of AM radio stations from FM competitors or private broadcasters from cable or cable from satellites, almost everyone involved in the broadcasting system rejects the traditional view of the market as the determinant of economic success and agrees on the appropriateness of a state agency to protect the various components of the industry from the United States and from each other.[37]

Over the years, successive Canadian governments have felt it justifiable to intervene in the mass media in a variety of ways. These interventions have often been controversial, both because they have been seen to endanger free expression and because they have benefited some groups at the expense of others. They have been, inevitably, tied to political forces and political priorities. They have also had varying degrees of success in achieving their intended goals. In general, because they have utilized primarily economic rather than cultural criteria, they have fostered industry rather than identity. Indeed, in many instances that has been the deliberate intention.

As has already been suggested, the future of regulation is in considerable doubt in this period of rapid technological and economic change in the media industries. Many of the new media, including satellites and especially the Internet, are less susceptible to regulation for simple technical reasons. Now that messages can cross borders straight into the homes of Canadians without the intervention of any Canadian common carrier, the possibilities for regulating the cultural industries — either the carriers or the messages — is severely reduced. "Open borders" are a reality.

Moreover, the process begun under American leadership after the Second World War toward freer world trade has accelerated in the last decade and has probably reached a point of no return. Because in its own self-interest the United States insists on a definition of media products as commodities and services just like any others, the protections that a number of countries — including Canada — have traditionally afforded their cultural industries for reasons of national unity and identity are under siege. Not only American officials but many Canadian economists, lobbyists and industry spokespeople support the argument that all barriers to free market development are wrong, wasteful and counter-productive.

The government is apparently listening to such arguments with an increasing amount of sympathy. Unfortunately, our rules and regulations have often helped to create cultural industries that are highly concentrated, very profitable for the fortunate few who own them, and not really committed to reflecting any social or national goals. It is at least in part out of a concern for the lack of diversity in ownership among Canadian daily newspapers, for example, that the Minister of Canadian Heritage has recently announced a re-thinking of the policies that prevent foreign ownership. This of course has occurred in the context of the announcement by the two major Canadian owners that they plan to sell many of their holdings; needless to say they enthusiastically support the possibility that they might be open to bids from across the border. Another reason for the government's willingness to reconsider many of its traditional cultural policies is in fact partly an outgrowth of their success. Entrepreneurs like Conrad Black and Ted Rogers and others have made enough money in the Canadian market that they have expanded — or are looking to expand — abroad. Similarly, the government-sponsored growth of the Canadian film, TV and video production industry in the last decade has led to considerable sales in foreign markets. But there comes a point when the ability to flog Canadian products overseas is blocked by reciprocal or retaliatory measures by other countries which resent their lack of full access to our market. In other words, according to this line of thinking, free trade works both ways, and insofar as Canada continues to impose barriers at home, Canadian opportunities elsewhere will be jeopardized. The Canadian loss at the WTO in the *Sports Illustrated* case is a sign of the new times; we will lose again on similar challenges — maybe not always, but often enough to force some re-thinking. As two distinguished experts in the economics of communications put it recently:

> While protectionist support may have been appropriate when the cultural industries could claim infant status, it is no longer justifiable. The Canadian industry is no longer an infant. In Canada and the rest of the world, technological changes have expanded trade and altered ownership and contractual relation-

ships among producers. With the greater wealth potential of the international market for cultural products, policies that pursue access abroad while restricting it at home spawn trade disputes and retaliation. In the end, Canada will have to choose between reciprocal access and being locked into the current inward-looking policies ... The best way to promote Canadian creativity and culture is to build firms that are internationally competitive.[38]

Last, but by no means least in this context, it seems that some policy-makers are becoming aware of the indefensibility of the many inconsistencies and incongruities in Canadian cultural policy. Matthew Fraser sums it up very well:

At present the main problem with Canada's position vis-à-vis Hollywood is the lack of consistency and coherence in Canadian cultural policies. Canada does not heavily regulate the inflow of books or videocassettes, yet it imposes Canadian content quotas on television and radio. No restrictions are placed on the ownership of cinemas or video stores in Canada — hence Famous Players, Cineplex Odeon and Blockbuster do business with impunity. And yet ownership restrictions apply to television and radio stations and telephone companies [and indirectly to newspapers and magazines]. In short, Canada has a complex arsenal of restrictive policy instruments that show no discernible coherence: restriction of inflows, ownership rules, direct subsidies, cross-subsidization schemes, eviction of foreign firms, government ownership, and special treatment under trade agreements. If these policies were applied evenly across all the cultural sectors, the Canadian government could at least claim conceptual clarity and coherence of purpose. But no such coherence exists. Canada's policies are a jumble of tools that reflect muddling through, crisis management, bureaucratic gridlock, and favours to special pleading and vested interests.[39]

It is clear that the minister of Industry, the minister of Canadian Heritage, the CRTC, and other policy-making bodies are aware of and are reacting to all of these issues of the new millennium. The CRTC has probably moved the furthest so far, having opened up the telephone market in the early 1990s and satellite broadcasting in the latter part of the decade. After some years of study, in early 1999 the commission announced that although it realized that some of the content on the Internet could be defined as broadcasting, it chose to consider it merely as a complement to broadcasting, and, at least for the time being, to eschew Internet regulation. David Colville, vice-chairman of the CRTC, summarized the new approach very clearly to a parliamentary committee in February 2000. The commission's role, he said, is to manage "a delicate balance between achieving various social and cultural objectives and establishing an economically strong and competitive communications industry." It was clear from the rest of his speech, however, that the emphasis lay on the latter — the competitive — and not on the former — the cultural:

> A primary emphasis of the Commission over the past several years has been to actively support market-driven competition as the primary means to promote consumer choice, foster innovation in the development of new services, and new pricing options ... The Commission has put into place the policies that will promote sustainable competition in the telecommunications and broadcasting sectors so that Canada can compete in the global market. These have been carefully tailored to foster a healthy transition from a monopoly market to a competition-driven market that will bring benefits to consumers for years to come.[40]

While some of the language may be blunter than in the past, the general theme is consistent with the trend of the government's approach to cultural policy for many years. Despite the rhetoric to the contrary, the government's policy emphasis is on the industry rather than on the content; it is on Canadians as consumers, not as citizens. The fundamental ambivalence between protectionism and liberalism that has haunted Canadian cultural policy from its earliest days is being resolved, in the context of technological and economic convergence and globalization, in favour of the latter.

Conclusion

For those who believe it important that the Canadian mass media serve mainly as vehicles by which Canadians can share information, attitudes and ideas with one another, a study of their historical development is discouraging. Whenever economic and technological goals are in conflict with cultural ones, it seems, the former triumph. Government attempts at regulation or stimulation seem mainly to serve entrepreneurial goals. Out of the ambivalence inherent in the concept of "cultural industries" have come measures that at best help the industry, rarely the culture.

From the beginning, government cultural policy has been oriented toward improving distribution systems. The first stimulative policy, postal subsidies for Canadian publications, was clearly distribution-oriented; for many years it was the largest single subsidy program in the cultural field. Similarly, the main thrust of the Aird Report and other documents central to the creation of the CBC was toward constructing the high-powered broadcasting stations necessary for a coast-to-coast radio network, not the programming that might be available on that network. The same may be said of the development of CBC television in the 1950s, particularly the affiliate-station arrangement. In recent times, this tendency to give priority to distributive technology over content is illustrated by the way cable TV was initially regulated solely to protect the revenues of over-the-air broadcasters without regard for the cultural issues raised by the wholesale importation of American signals.

The reasons for this emphasis are not hard to identify. Given Canada's geographical and demographic configuration, communication systems have been critical to nation-building ever since Confederation. To enable the mass media to play their appropriate role in this challenging task, governments have felt that they must help widen audience access either through stimulation of private enterprise or, when that failed, through actual government ownership. When money was short — as it usually was — little was left over for content, even if liberal belief-systems had allowed active government intervention in the production of cultural and informational goods. This long-standing stress on expanding distribution systems has been seen by some scholars as a kind of Canadian technophilia — the product of an apparently ingrained belief in the magic power of the technology of communications to create and define the country.

But the susceptibility of Canadian governments to this sort of "technological nationalism" is not the whole explanation for the over-emphasis on the process of communication rather than substance.[1] Expanding media-distribution systems also served the goals of Canadian (and branch plant) businesses by offering them access to larger groups of consumers. Not only did media owners importune the government for aid in expanding their distributive capacity, so did Canadian advertisers. For neither of these groups was Canadian content of any particular relevance; their interest in content rested solely in its ability to attract large audiences of consumers as cheaply as possible.

The demands of ordinary Canadians must not be forgotten either. Beginning with the daily newspaper in the late nineteenth century, many Canadians have come to depend on the mass media for regular information and entertainment. They, too, have consistently supported government measures that made their favourite media more available at lower prices. Most critically, Canadian consumers have demanded equality of media access, as the cases of private television and cable indicate. There is little doubt that the governments in power in the late 1950s and late 1960s respectively, were pressured by consumer demand for the introduction first of all of "second stations" and then of American network signals on Canadian cable. The inherent inequity of a situation in which some Canadians could watch American television while others could not was politically indefensible. As Morris Wolfe put it, "Canadians who live outside Toronto have never had much love for the place, but they insist on their inalienable right to have what Torontonians have."[2] Out of the congruence of all these factors, then, has developed a situation in which media-distribution systems in Canada have expanded much more rapidly than the capacity to fill those systems with Canadian content.

In 1965 the Fowler Committee on Broadcasting opened its report with the statement: "The only thing that really matters in broadcasting is program content; all the rest is housekeeping."[3] The committee members were suggesting that cultural, not industrial, strategies should henceforth be the government's priority. The time had come, they felt, to place the emphasis on content, not distribution. In the 1980s, both the Applebaum-Hébert Policy Review Committee and the Caplan-Sauvageau Task Force repeated the same message. Both strongly supported the CBC for this reason, for example, because they understood that nowhere else on television was Canadian content a priority.

But what has actually happened in the thirty-five years since the Fowler Committee coined its famous aphorism? The CBC has been subject to regular budget cuts and its audience has shrunk. Cable brings all the American networks into 75 per cent of Canadian homes. Pay-TV channels have been given only minimal Canadian content requirements, which the CRTC reduces at the slightest hint of financial difficulty (although most specialty channels do have quite high Cancon minimums). One positive step has been the introduction of the Broadcast Program Development Fund, but even that is nowhere nearly adequate to provide the amount of high-quality Canadian programming the system needs.

The situation is similar in the other mass media. Despite much wringing of hands and appointment of royal commissions, few concrete solutions have been found to pressing problems. Canadian cinemas remain an almost wholly foreign venue; Canadian magazines, desperately struggling to survive postal rate increases, the GST, and the potential loss of advertising from the split-run decision, are barely visible on our newsstands; newspaper ownership is concentrated in fewer and fewer hands.

This pattern is not an accident, but neither is it simply the result of the "capture" of government cultural administrators by business interests. It is the product of a number of the fundamental convictions which both ordinary Canadians and their governments have consistently shared: that private enterprise is the principal motor of our economy, that a press free of government involvement is essential to democracy, that all Canadians deserve equal treatment, and that because of its geographic and population diversity, Canada needs an advanced communications system. Given the broadly based nature of this belief-system, the social and political will to rescue the Canadian mass media from their ambiguous status does not seem to exist.

As new technologies and global economic competition change the nature of the media business in the twenty-first century, however, a thorough reassessment of Canada's position and the assumptions on which it is based must be undertaken. Certain realities constrain our choices. It is only feasible to assume, for example, that because of the historical development and present situation of our media, private enterprise will remain the normal mode of ownership and operation. In that context, it will continue to be necessary to allow Canadian media owners to make a fair return on their investments. Equally, at this point the access of ordinary Canadians to American media cannot be substantially reduced. The highly polished products of the American television, film and magazine industries are very popular in Canada; ingrained habits and preferences cannot be easily overridden.

Nevertheless, better ways must be found to ensure that Canadian alternatives also exist. The banning of imported products is unacceptable, but stimulation of the creation of local works, by quotas or other devices, is quite legitimate. As innumerable commentators have pointed out, Canadians should at least be offered the choice of their own cultural goods. This sort of concentrated effort to address questions of media content will demand that the Canadian people and their government lose their traditional reluctance to require performance standards of entrepreneurs in the cultural industries. While under traditional liberal assumptions the media received hands-off treatment because of their special nature, in fact that unique role is the very reason that intervention is essential, particularly in the changing world context. Cultural policymakers must be less tentative and better focussed in using the levers of government to promote the use of material which is both created by Canadian cultural producers and which meets the diverse needs of Canadian consumers. They must lose their obsession with business and technology, and promote culture.

There are certain hopeful signs. The CRTC's decision in the early 1990s to tie Canadian-content requirements to station profitability and to specify program categories was a move in the right direction. So was the decision to place Canadian specialty services on basic cable, giving them the edge over imported channels. While the reduction in postal subsidies and the diversion of advertising revenues to split-run magazines is to be regretted, a targeted direct-grants program for magazines and newspapers can better serve cultural as well as industrial ends. Similarly, Telefilm funding, although frozen, seems to have better results than the CCA tax break policy ever did. But much more could be done. Stronger content requirements for pay-TV and satellite services could easily be put in place. The film distribution bill could be reintroduced. Perhaps most imperative, a strong new mandate for the CBC must be designed. The corporation's past attempt to be all things to all people needs to be seriously reconsidered in an age of narrowcasting, so that the publicly owned broadcaster can provide a more specialized service which is a genuine alternative to the other kinds of programming available.

For private film and television producers, the multi-channel world of the future will undoubtedly spell opportunity. Already, Canadian firms are making many international sales and co-production arrangements owing to the opening up of unprecedented distribution opportunities on specialty channels around the world, including the United States (where our cultural similarity may even be a bonus). Although some still cry doom and gloom, and American dominance of world media markets is not about to vanish, the outlook for industrial development in this sector seems to be very positive. But what of its cultural side? Some would argue that almost by definition co-productions lose any identifiable Canadian character, that they contribute nothing to the ability of Canadians to talk to one another. Others would counter that any growth in the industry is valuable, because it develops talent, money and creativity that may cross-subsidize more purely domestic-oriented production as well.

The ability and willingness of the federal government to act in the area of media content depends very much on the pressure it receives from the public. Most Canadians are largely passive consumers of cultural products. They need to be made more aware of the personal, social and national importance of all the millions of words and images they absorb — perhaps by means of more school courses that teach children how to "read" film and television as they are taught how to read books. Canadians also must be more conscious of the negative consequences for "marginal" countries of the laissez-faire approach to media control and content, and that American assumptions about the role of the media in society are not wholly applicable here. Vigilance is particularly necessary at the present time, as we face a new media environment where many traditional kinds of controls are no longer feasible. We must rethink government policy with reference to all our cultural industries. Measures instituted in the 1970s are no longer relevant. But in the course of that rethinking, we must also never lose our focus on what our priorities should be. As the debate about "electronic colonialism" continues at the international level in the coming years, so will the debate about Canada's media dilemmas continue here. This country has already confronted, rather unsuccessfully, the problem of how to maintain national cultural goals in an environment of very unequal competition with the mass-media giant of the world. It will continue to confront new challenges posed by the simultaneous trends to fragmentation, globalization and the new media. Canadians must continue imaginatively to seek the right balance between cultural needs and economic realities.

Notes

Introduction

1. J.L. Granatstein, *Yankee Go Home?: Canadians and anti-Americanism* (Toronto, HarperCollins, 1996), p. 217; *Globe and Mail*, February 12, 1997, p. A10.
2. Robert Fulford, "Communications," *Canadian Encyclopedia*, 2nd ed., (Edmonton: Hurtig, 1988), Vol. 1, p. 469.
3. Karl W. Deutsch, *Nationalism and Social Communication: An Inquiry into the Foundations of Nationality*, 2nd ed. (Cambridge, Mass.: M.I.T. Press, 1966), p. 97.
4. The word myth is used in the sense of a set of images and symbols that shape the world view of a group.
4. See Emily S. Rosenberg, *Spreading the American Dream: American Economic and Cultural Expansion, 1890–1945* (New York: Hill and Wang, 1982), p. 7.
6. See, for example, Allan Smith, "The Continental Dimension in the Evolution of the English-Canadian Mind," in his *Canada — an American Nation?: Essays on Continentalism, Identity, and the Canadian Frame of Mind* (Montreal and Kingston: McGill-Queen's University Press, 1994), pp. 40-64.

Chapter 1: The Rise of the Mass Media

1. Cited in B.P.N. Beaven, "'Anxious, Vexed, or Harassed': Philip Dansken Ross 'Making It' as a Working Journalist in the 1880's," unpublished paper delivered to Canadian Historical Association meeting, 1988.
2. See Bruce Curtis, "Preconditions of the Canadian State: Educational Reform and the Construction of a Public in Upper Canada, 1837-1846," *Studies in Political Economy*, 10 (1983), pp. 111–12.
3. Quoted in Hugh Cunningham, *Leisure in the Industrial Revolution, c. 1780–c. 1880* (London: Croom Helm, 1980), p. 150.
4. See Paul Rutherford, "The People's Press: The Emergence of the New Journalism in Canada, 1869–99," *Canadian Historical Review*, 56 (1975), pp. 169–91.
5. Paul Rutherford, *A Victorian Authority: The Daily Press in Late Nineteenth-Century Canada* (Toronto: University of Toronto Press, 1982), pp. 53–56.
6. Jean de Bonville, *La presse québécoise de 1884 à 1914: Genèse d'un média de masse* (Québec: Les presses de l'Université Laval, 1988), p. 232.

7. Minko Sotiron, *From Politics to Profit: The Commercialization of Canadian Daily Newspapers, 1890-1920* (Montreal and Kingston: McGill-Queen's University Press, 1997), pp. 115–24.

8. B.P.N. Beaven, "Partisanship, Patronage, and the Press in Ontario, 1880-1914: Myths and Realities," *Canadian Historical Review,* 64 (1983), p. 349.

9. Figures cited in Sotiron, p. 24.

10. H.E. Stephenson and Carleton McNaught, *The Story of Advertising in Canada: A Chronicle of Fifty Years* (Toronto: Ryerson Press, 1940), p. 3.

11. *A Victorian Authority,* p. 98.

12. See Dallas W. Smythe, *Dependency Road: Communications, Capitalism, Conciousness, and Canada* (Norwood, N.J.: Ablex Publishing Corp., 1981).

13. Raymond Williams, "The Existing Alternatives in Communications," in K.J. McGarry, ed., *Mass Communications* (London: Bingley, 1972), pp. 60–61.

14. Quoted in Sotiron, p. 51.

15. See Theodore Peterson, *Magazines in the Twentieth Century* (Urbana: University of Illinois Press, 1964), p. 13.

16. Samuel Moffett, *The Americanization of Canada* (Toronto: University of Toronto Press, 1972; first published 1907), p. 100.

Chapter 2: The Media and Canadian Nationalism: 1920-1950

1. Editorial, "National Periodicals or Annexation," *Saturday Night* (March 20, 1926), p. 2.

2. Canada, House of Commons, *Debates,* July 17, 1931, p. 3889.

3. I. Litvak and C. Maule, *Cultural Sovereignty: The Time and Reader's Digest Case in Canada* (New York: Praeger, 1974), p. 26; Canada, House of Commons, *Debates,* March 13, 1936, p. 1151.

4. Peter Morris, *Embattled Shadows: A History of Canadian Cinema, 1895-1939* (Montreal: McGill-Queen's University Press, 1978), p. 26.

5. M. Pendakur, *Canadian Dreams and American Control: The Political Economy of the Canadian Film Industry* (Toronto: Garamond Press, 1990), pp. 63–70, 87–94.

6. See Pierre Berton, *Hollywood's Canada: The Americanization of our National Image* (Toronto: McClelland and Stewart, 1975).

7. Quoted in Y. Lamonde et P.-F. Hébert, *Le Cinéma au Québec: Essai de statistique historique (1895 à nos jours)* (Montréal: Institut Québécois de Recherche sur la Culture, 1981), p. 28.

8. Régie du Cinéma du Québec Website, www.mcc.gouv.gc.ca/orgasoc/regicine; accessed April 2, 2000.

9. Pendakur, pp. 83–85.

10. Quoted in Morris, p. 181.

11. Berton, pp. 189–91.

12. P. Morris, "Backwards to the Future: John Grierson's Film Policy for Canada," in Gene Walz, ed., *Flashback: People and Institutions in Canadian Film History*, Canadian Film Studies, 2 (Montreal: Mediatexte Publications Inc., 1986), pp. 19–26.

13. See Joyce Nelson, *The Colonized Eye: Rethinking the Grierson Legend* (Toronto: Between the Lines, 1988).

14. See Mary Vipond, *Listening In: The First Decade of Canadian Broadcasting, 1922–1932* (Montreal: McGill-Queen's University Press, 1992).

15. Royal Commission on National Development in the Arts, Letters and Sciences, 1949–1951 (Massey Commission), *Report* (Ottawa: King's Printer, 1951), p. 281.

16. *Ibid.*, pp. 449, 477.

17. On radio in Quebec in this period, see Michel Filion, *Radiodiffusion et société distincte: Des origines de la radio jusqu'à la Révolution tranquille au Québec* (Laval, Québec: Méridien, 1994).

18. S. M. Trofimenkoff, *Action Française: French Canadian Nationalism in the Twenties* (Toronto: University of Toronto Press, 1975), p. 76.

19. Massey *Report*, pp. 4–5.

20. See Paul Litt, *The Muses, the Masses, and the Massey Commission* (Toronto: University of Toronto Press, 1992), especially Chapter 6.

Chapter 3: The Television Age

1. Quoted in Paul Rutherford, *When Television Was Young: Primetime Canada 1952–1967* (Toronto: University of Toronto Press, 1990), p. 121.

2. Frank Peers, *The Public Eye: Television and the Politics of Canadian Broadcasting, 1952–68* (Toronto: University of Toronto Press, 1979), p. 223.

3. Quoted in *ibid.*, p. 303.

4. Data on television viewing in this paragraph is from the Statistics Canada Website, www.statcan.ca/english/Pgdb/PeopleCulture/arts/; accessed April 13, 2000.

5. Television Bureau of Canada Website, www.tvb.ca/TVBasicsPublic99-00; accessed April 13, 2000.

6. Report of the Task Force on Broadcasting Policy (Caplan-Sauvageau Report) (Ottawa: Minister of Supply and Services, 1986), pp. 81, 91–97.

7. David Ellis, *Networking* (Toronto: Friends of Canadian Broadcasting, 1991), p. 21.

8. Matthew Fraser, *Free-for-All: The Struggle for Dominance on the Digital Frontier* (Toronto: Stoddart, 1999), pp. 183-4.

9. Y. Lamonde et P.-F. Hébert, *Le Cinéma au Québec: Essai de statistique historique (1895 à nos jours)* (Montréal: Institut Québécois de Recherche sur la Culture, 1981) p. 42.

10. Paul Audley, *Canada's Cultural Industries: Broadcasting, Publishing, Records and Film* (Toronto: James Lorimer, 1983) p. 215.

11. Tom McSorley, "Critical Mass: Thirty Years of Telefilm Canada," *Take One* (Winter, 1999), p. 30.

12. I. Litvak and C. Maule, *Cultural Sovereignty: The Time and Reader's Digest Case in Canada* (New York: Praeger, 1984) pp. 30–31.

13. Order-in-Council P.C. 1960-1270, Sept. 16, 1960.

14. See Litvak and Maule, p. 72; Special Senate Committee on Mass Media (Davey Committee), Vol. 1, *The Uncertain Mirror* (Ottawa: Minister of Supply and Services, 1970), p. 162; and Denis Smith, *Gentle Patriot: A Political Biography of Walter Gordon* (Edmonton: Hurtig, 1973), p. 232.

15. Litvak and Maule, pp. 91–92.

16. Davey Committee, pp. 153, 163.

17. For an interesting analysis of the political forces that lay behind the introduction of Bill C-58 see Sylvia Bashevkin, *True Patriot Love: The Politics of Canadian Nationalism* (Toronto: Oxford University Press, 1991), p. 74ff.

18. Steven Globerman, *Culture, Governments and Markets: Public Policy and the Culture Industries* (Vancouver: The Fraser Institute, 1987), p. 35.

19. Val Ross, "Saturday Night Promotion Confirmed," Toronto *Globe and Mail*, March 19, 1992, p. C5.

20. See John Miller, *Yesterday's News: Why Canada's Daily Newspapers are Failing Us* (Halifax, Fernwood Publishing, 1998).

21. Royal Commission on Newspapers (Kent Report) (Ottawa: Minister of Supply and Services, 1981), p. 215.

22. Competitors have since re-entered two of these markets, the Toronto Sun Corporation's Ottawa *Sun* and Quebecor's Winnipeg *Sun*.

23. Kent Report, p. 217.

24. See for example, Peter Desbarats, *Guide to Canadian News Media* (Toronto: Harcourt Brace Jovanovich, Canada, 1990), pp. 72–73; N. Russell, "Staffing Levels as a Reflector of Quality," *Canadian Journal of Communication*, 16 (1991), pp. 118–28; Robert G. Picard, *Media Economics: Concepts and Issues* (Newbury Park, California: Sage, 1989), pp. 79–80; Miller, Part One.

Chapter 4: The Economics of the Mass Media

1. See Dallas Smythe, *Dependency Road: Communications, Capitalism, Consciousness, and Canada* (Norwood, N.J.: Ablex Publishing Corporation, 1981).

2. Royal Commission on Newspapers (Kent Report), (Ottawa: Minister of Supply and Services, 1981), p. 98.

3. Richard Collins, *Culture, Communication and National Identity: The Case of Canadian Television* (Toronto: University of Toronto Press, 1990), p. 100.

4. David Ellis, *Networking* (Toronto: Friends of Canadian Broadcasting, 1991), p. 140.

5. Report of the Task Force on Broadcasting Policy (Caplan-Sauvageau) (Ottawa: Minister of Supply and Services, 1986), p. 433.

6. Ellis, p. 141.

7. CTV was consolidated under the control of Baton Broadcasting with Ivan Fecan as CEO in 1998. On Global's Canadian content, see Matthew

Fraser, *Free-for-All: The Struggle for Dominance on the Digital Frontier* (Toronto: Stoddart, 1999), p. 168.

8. Peter Desbarats, *Guide to Canadian News Media* (Toronto: Harcourt Brace Jovanovich, Canada, 1990), p. 115.

9. John Miller, *Yesterday's News: Why Canada's Daily Newspapers are Failing Us* (Halifax: Fernwood, 1998), p. 66.

10. For more information on the Canadian sound recording industry, see Paul Audley, *Canada's Cultural Industries* (Toronto: James Lorimer, 1983), Chapter 4 and Will Straw, "Sound Recording," in Michael Dorland, ed., *The Cultural Industries in Canada: Problems, Policies and Prospects* (Toronto: James Lorimer, 1996).

11. Quoted in Kent Report, p. 72.

12. Much of this argument is based on Bruce M. Owen, *Economics and Freedom of Expression: Media Structure and the First Amendment* (Cambridge, Mass.: Ballinger, 1975), pp. 12–18.

13. Time Digital Website, www.time.com/time/digital/digital 50/; accessed April 21, 2000.

14. Thelma McCormack, "The Political Culture and the Press of Canada," *Canadian Journal of Political Science*, XVI (1983), p. 455.

15. Audley, p. 60.

16. Erik Barnouw, *The Image Empire*, Vol. 3 of *A History of Broadcasting in the United States* (New York: Oxford University Press, 1970) p. 23; Ben H. Bagdikian, *The Media Monopoly*, 2nd ed. (Boston: Beacon Press, 1987), pp. 167, 171; Barrie Zwicker, "Where commerce, journalism meet," Toronto *Globe and Mail*, September 15, 1990, pp. D1, D8.

17. Senate Committee on Mass Media (Davey Report), Vol. 1, *The Uncertain Mirror* (Ottawa: Minister of Supply and Services, 1970), p. 243.

18. Owen, p. 19.

19. James Curran and Jean Seaton, *Power Without Responsibility: The Press and Broadcasting in Britain* (Glasgow: Fontana Paperbacks, 1981), p. 17.

20. Avrim Lazar and Associates, Ltd., *Attitudes of Canadians Toward Advertising and Television* (Ottawa: Minister of Supply and Services, 1978), pp. 32–33.

21. A. Rotstein, "The Use and Misuse of Economics in Cultural Policy," in R. Lorimer and D. Wilson, eds., *Communication Canada: Issues in Broadcasting and New Technologies* (Toronto: Kagan and Woo, 1988), p. 149.

22. Steven Globerman, *Cultural Regulation in Canada* (Montreal: The Institute for Research in Public Policy, 1983), p. xxiii. See also Steven Globerman, "Competition and Regulatory Policies for the I-Way," *Policy Options* (October 1996), pp. 11-15.

23. Globerman, *Cultural Regulation in Canada*, p. xx.

24. Steven Globerman, *Culture, Governments and Markets* (Vancouver: The Fraser Institute, 1987), p. 22.

25. For a brief summary, see Rotstein's article cited above and, in the same volume, David Mitchell, "Culture and Political Discourse in Canada."

26. Collins, pp. 145–46.

27. Report of the Federal Cultural Policy Review Committee (Applebaum-Hébert Report) (Ottawa: Minister of Supply and Services, 1982), p. 68.

28. Rotstein, pp. 155–56.

Chapter 5: Culture and the Mass Media

1. Michael Real, *Mass-Mediated Culture* (Englewood Cliffs, N.J.: Prentice-Hall, 1977), p. 10.

2. Quoted in Barrie Zwicker, "Reflections on the Kent Report," in B. Zwicker and D. MacDonald, eds., *News: Inside the Canadian Media* (Ottawa: Deneau, 1982), p. 294.

3. This is the classic definition of E.B. Tyler. See A.L. Kroeber and C. Kluckhohn, *Culture: A Critical Review of Concepts and Definitions* (New York: Random House, Vintage Edition, 1963), p. 81.

4. A. Rotstein, "The Use and Misuse of Economics in Cultural Policy," in R. Lorimer and D. Wilson, eds., *Communication Canada: Issues in Broadcasting and New Technologies* (Toronto: Kagan and Woo, 1988), p. 144.

5. M. Raboy *et al.*, "Cultural Development and the Open Economy: A Democratic Issue and a Challenge to Public Policy," *Canadian Journal of Communication*, 19 (1994), p. 303.

6. Unless otherwise noted, material in this section is derived mainly from the following texts: Denis McQuail, *Mass Communication Theory: An Introduction* (London: Sage Publications, 1983); M. Gurevitch, T. Bennett, J. Curran and J. Woollacott, eds., *Mass Communication and Society* (London: Edward Arnold, 1977); and Ross A. Eamon, *The Media Society: Basic Issues and Controversies* (Toronto: Butterworths, 1987).

7. N. Vidmar and M. Rokeach, "Archie Bunker's Bigotry: A Study in Selective Perception and Exposure," *Journal of Communication*, 24 (1974), p. 46.

8. J.W. Carey, "Mass Communication Research and Cultural Studies: An American View," in Curran *et al.*, p. 412.

9. J.W. Carey, "A Cultural Approach to Communication," in *Communication as Culture: Essays on Media and Society* (Boston: Unwin Hyman, 1988), p. 18.

10. *Ibid.*, pp. 20–21.

11. Raymond Williams, "Base and Superstructure in Marxist Cultural Theory," *New Left Review*, 82 (November-December 1973), pp. 3–16.

12. Stuart Hall, "Culture, the Media and the 'Ideological Effect,' " in Curran *et al.*, p. 346.

13. Real, p. 4.

14. This section is based on the following sources: Anthony Smith, *The Geopolitics of Information: How Western Culture Dominates the World* (London, Faber and Faber, 1980); International Commission for the Study of Communication Problems (MacBride Report), *Many Voices, One World* (UNESCO, 1980); George Gerbner and M. Siefert, eds., *World Communications: A Handbook* (New York: Longman, 1984); J. Tunstall, *The Media*

Are American (New York: Columbia University Press, 1977); J. Becker, G. Hedebro and L. Paldan, eds., *Communication and Domination: Essays to Honor Herbert I. Schiller* (Norwood, N.J.: Ablex Publishing Corporation, 1986); Thomas L. McPhail, *Electronic Colonialism: The Future of International Broadcasting and Communication* (Newbury Park, Calif.: Sage Publications, 1987) and Peter Golding and Phil Harris, eds., *Beyond Cultural Imperialism: Globalization, Communication and the New International Order*, (London: Sage, 1997).

15. H.I. Schiller, *Culture, Inc.: The Corporate Takeover of Public Expression* (New York: Oxford University Press, 1989), pp. 137–38.

16. Cited in Morris Wolfe, "Despite the crunch, there are things the CBC still must do," Toronto *Globe and Mail*, December 20, 1990, p. C1.

17. Smith, p. 43.

18. M. Masmoudi, "The New World Information Order," in Gerbner and Siefert, p. 16.

19. E. Katz and T. Liebes, "Once Upon a Time, in Dallas," *Intermedia*, 12 (May 1984), pp. 28–32.

20. G. Valaskakis, "Communication and Control in the Canadian North: The Inuit Experience," in B. Singer, ed., *Communications in Canadian Society* (Don Mills: Addison-Wesley, 1983) p. 241.

21. Colleen Roach, "The Movement for a New World Information and Communication Order: A Second Wave?" *Media, Culture and Society*, 12 (1990), p. 294.

22. Benjamin Barber, *Jihad vs. McWorld* (New York: Times Books, 1995).

23. R.-J. Ravault, "Des effets pervers de l'expansion mondiale des médias américains," pp. 226–51 and C.-J. Bertrand, "L'Impérialisme culturel américain, un mythe?" pp. 20–24, both in C.-J. Bertrand et F. Bordat, éds., *Les Médias Américains en France* (n.p.: Belin, 1989).

24. F.S. Siebert, T. Peterson and W. Schramm, *Four Theories of the Press* (Urbana: University of Illinois Press, 1956).

25. McPhail, p. 165.

26. Roach, p. 298.

27. Editorial, "Rationing 'Dallas' in Europe," New York *Times*, October 24, 1989, p. A26.

28. Ted Magder, "Going Global," *Canadian Forum* (August 1999), p. 13.

29. See for example Colleen Roach, "The Western World and the NWICO: United They Stand?", in Peter Golding and Phil Harris, eds., especially pp. 106-7.

30. Smith, pp. 52–57; see also McPhail, pp. 24–32.

31. Royal Commission on Publications (O'Leary), *Report* (Ottawa: Queen's Printer, 1961), p. 4.

32. M. Atwood, *Survival* (Toronto: Anansi, 1972), p. 19.

33. Paul Audley, "Cultural Industries Policy: Objectives, Formulation, and Evaluation," *Canadian Journal of Communication*, 19 (1994), p. 318.

34. See, for example, D. Hall and A. Siegel, "The Impact of Social Forces on the Canadian Media," in Singer, p. 66; Morris Wolfe, *Jolts: The TV Wasteland and the Canadian Oasis* (Toronto: James Lorimer, 1985), and André

Gosselin *et al.*, "Violence on Canadian Television and Some of its Cognitive Effects," *Canadian Journal of Communication*, 22 (1997), pp. 143–160.

35. Richard Collins, *Culture, Communication and National Identity* (Toronto: University of Toronto Press, 1990), pp. 299–300.

36. Quoted in Frank Peers, *The Public Eye* (Toronto: University of Toronto Press, 1979), p. 42.

37. Quoted in Frank Peers, "Oh, say, can you see?" in I. Lumsden, ed., *Close the 49th Parallel, etc.* (Toronto: University of Toronto Press, 1970) p. 13.

38. Paul Rutherford, *The Making of the Canadian Media* (Toronto: McGraw-Hill Ryerson, 1978), p. 102.

39. H.F. Angus, ed., *Canada and her Great Neighbor: Sociological Surveys of Opinions and Attitudes in Canada Concerning the United States* (New York: 1938; reissued by Russell and Russell), p. 400.

40. Doug Camilli, Montreal *Gazette*, Sept. 25, 1986, p. D-8.

41. For example, see those of 1970 and 1980 cited in Collins, pp. 86, 234, and those of the late 1980s cited in David Ellis, *Networking* (Toronto: Friends of Canadian Broadcasting, 1991), p. 163.

42. Quoted in Canadian Association for Adult Education, *Voices of Concern: The Future of Canadian Broadcasting* (n.p., n.d), p. 1.

43. W.T. Stanbury, "Cancon Rules Should be Canned," *Policy Options* (October 1996), p. 25.

44. Richard Schultz, "Canadian Content and the I-Way," *Policy Options* (October 1996), p. 11.

45. Keith Acheson and Christopher Maule, "Canada's Cultural Policies — You Can't Have it Both Ways," *Canadian Foreign Policy*, 4 (Winter 1997), pp. 65-81; Doug Saunders, "A Cheater's Guide to Canadian Television," *Globe and Mail*, October 23, 1999, pp. C1-C2.

46. Matthew Fraser, *Free-for-All: The Struggle for Dominance of the Digital Frontier* (Toronto: Stoddart, 1999), p. xvi.

47. Arthur Siegel, *Politics and the Media in Canada* (Toronto: McGraw-Hill Ryerson, 1983), p. 178.

48. Marc Raboy, *Missed Opportunities: The Story of Canada's Broadcasting Policy* (Montreal: McGill-Queen's University Press, 1990), pp. xii, 339.

49. Rutherford, *Making of Canadian Media*, p. 103.

50. Collins, pp. 4, 13.

51. Montreal *Gazette*, Oct. 21, 1986, p. A2.

52. Friends of Canadian Broadcasting Website, www.friendscb.org/polls/CBCmay1999; accessed April 20, 2000.

53. I. Litvak and C. Maule, *Cultural Sovereignty: The Time and Reader's Digest Case in Canada* (New York: Praeger, 1974), p. 34.

54. David Rothkop, "In Praise of Cultural Imperialism?" *Foreign Policy* (Summer 1997), pp. 39, 46.

55. J. Meisel, "Stroking the Airwaves: The Regulation of Broadcasting by the CRTC," in B.D. Singer, ed., *Communications in Canadian Society*, 3rd ed. (Toronto: Nelson, 1991), p. 227.

56. Friends of Canadian Broadcasting Website, www.friendscb.org/polls/ CBCmay1999; accessed April 20, 2000.

Chapter 6: Technology and the Mass Media

1. Described in "Catching Up with Videotron," *Broadcaster*, 42 (April 1983), p. 25.

2. John Howkins quoted in T.L. McPhail, *Electronic Colonialism: The Future of International Broadcasting and Communication* (Newbury Park, Calif.: Sage Publications, 1987), p. 151.

3. This framework is developed in Ross Eaman, *The Mass Society: Basic Issues and Controversies* (Toronto: Butterworths, 1987), pp. 150–60, and is a variant of that of Michel Benamou.

4. Quoted in Joyce Nelson, *The Perfect Machine: TV in the Nuclear Age* (Toronto: Between the Lines, 1987), p. 11.

5. Harold Innis, *The Fur Trade in Canada: An Introduction to Economic History* (Toronto: University of Toronto Press, rev. ed., 1956), p. 393.

6. Carl Berger, *The Writing of Canadian History: Aspects of English-Canadian Historical Writing 1900–1970* (Toronto: Oxford University Press, 1976), pp. 98–99.

7. J. W. Carey, "Harold Adams Innis and Marshall McLuhan," in R. Rosenthal, ed., *McLuhan: Pro and Con* (Baltimore: Penguin Books, 1969), p. 273.

8. Berger, pp. 102, 103.

9. Report of the Task Force on Broadcasting Policy (Caplan-Sauvageau Report) (Ottawa: Minister of Supply and Services, 1986), p. 76.

10. George Grant, *Lament for a Nation: The Defeat of Canadian Nationalism* (Toronto: McClelland and Stewart, 1965), p. 76.

11. Caplan-Sauvageau Report, p. 104.

12. E.F. Einsieldel and S. Green, "VCRs in Canada: Usage Patterns and Policy Implications," *Canadian Journal of Communication*, 13 (Winter 1988), pp. 30–31.

13. Mike Boone, "Your Own Instant Replays," Montreal *Gazette*, August 14, 1999, p. B4.

14. Quoted in Caplan-Sauvageau Report, p. 606.

15. Matthew Fraser, *Free-for-All: The Struggle for Dominance on the Digital Frontier* (Toronto: Stoddart, 1999), p. 28. In addition to specific quotations, I am indebted to Fraser's general argument in this and the next chapter.

16. *Ibid.*, p. 258.

17. *Ibid.*, p. 125.

18. Sean Maloney of Intel Corp., quoted in Mark Evans, "Web surfing on TV? Bad bet, Intel VP says," *Globe and Mail*, February 9, 2000, p. B1.

19. These were the predictions of Daniel Lamarre, Chair of the Board of the Canadian Association of Broadcasters (CAB), on introducing the CAB's 2000-2005 Strategic Plan, March 28, 2000; CAB Website, www.cab-acr.ca/english/joint/statements/speech_mar2800; accessed April 13, 2000.

20. Jeffrey Simpson, "The Great Canadian Television Challenge," *Globe and Mail*, March 10, 2000, p. A11.

21. D. MacDonald and F. Rumsey, "Pay-Triation — Fulfilling a Canadian Promise," in R.B. Woodrow and K.B. Woodside, eds., *The Introduction of Pay-TV in Canada* (Montreal: The Institute for Research in Public Policy, 1982), pp. 161-2.

22. Caplan-Sauvageau Report, p. 75.

Chapter 7: The Government and the Mass Media

1. R. Everett and F.J. Fletcher, "The Mass Media and Political Communication in Canada," in B.D. Singer, ed., *Communications in Canadian Society*, 3rd ed. (Toronto: Nelson, 1991), p. 165.

2. A good case study of this phenomenon is David Taras, "Television and Public Policy: The CBC's Coverage of the Meech Lake Accord," *Canadian Public Policy*, XV (1989), 322-34.

3. David Taras, *The Newsmakers: The Media's Influence on Canadian Politics* (Toronto: Nelson, 1990), pp. 235-7; Peter Desbarats, *Guide to Canadian News Media* (Toronto: Harcourt Brace Jovanovich, Canada, 1990), pp. 132, 147.

4. Everett and Fletcher, p. 178.

5. See J. McNulty, "Technology and Nation-building in Canadian Broadcasting," in R. Lorimer and D. Wilson, eds., *Communication Canada: Issues in Broadcasting and New Technologies* (Toronto: Kagan and Woo, 1988), p. 186.

6. Quoted in Montreal *Gazette*, Nov. 10, 1987, p. B7.

7. For lengthy and ongoing discussion of many aspects of Canadian broadcasting and especially the role of the CBC, see the Friends' Website at www.friendscb.org.

8. M. Raboy, *Missed Opportunities* (Montreal: McGill-Queen's University Press, 1990), p. 11.

9. Department of Communications, *Vital Links: Canadian Cultural Industries* (Ottawa: Minister of Supply and Services, 1987), p. 38.

10. Report of the Special Senate Committee on the Mass Media (Davey Committee), Vol. 1, *The Uncertain Mirror* (Ottawa: Minister of Supply and Services, 1970), p. 238.

11. Tom McSorley, "Critical Mass: Thirty Years of Telefilm Canada," *Take One* (Winter 1999), p. 29.

12. P. Audley, *Canada's Cultural Industries* (Toronto: James Lorimer, 1983), p. 302.

13. Steven Globerman, *Cultural Regulation in Canada* (Montreal: Institute for Research on Public Policy, 1983), p. 77. See also Wyndham Wise, "Boom to Bust: The Tax-Shelter Years," *Take One* (Winter 1999), pp. 17-24.

14. Maurie Alioff quoted in K. Acheson and C. Maule, "It Seemed Like a Good Idea at the Time," *Canadian Journal of Communication*, 16 (1991), p. 266.

15. Matthew Fraser, *Free-for-All: The Struggle for Dominance on the Digital Frontier* (Toronto: Stoddart, 1999), p. 252.

16. Acheson and Maule, pp. 263-76.

17. David Ellis, *Networking* (Toronto: Friends of Canadian Broadcasting, 1991), p. 200.

18. Audley, p. 244.

19. R.E. Babe and C. Winn, *Broadcasting Policy and Copyright Law: An Analysis of a Cable Rediffusion Right* (Ottawa: Department of Communications, 1984), pp. 3-6.

20. For details, see Stephen Godfrey, "Behind the Big Screen," Toronto *Globe and Mail*, March 28, 1992, pp. A1, A6.

21. Graham Carr, "Trade Liberalization and the Political Economy of Culture: An International Perspective on FTA," *Canadian-American Public Policy*, Number 6 (June 1991), 28; Vincent Mosco, "Toward a Transnational World Information Order: The Canada-U.S. Free Trade Agreement," *Canadian Journal of Communication*, 15 (1990), p. 49.

22. Ted Magder, "Going Global," *Canadian Forum* (August 1999), p. 15.

23. *Ibid.*, p. 16.

24. Editorial, "Magazine Hand-Outs," *Globe and Mail*, August 17, 1999, p. A12.

25. Marie Finkelstein, "Selected Social Issues in Programming: The Legal, Constitutional and Policy Implications of the Equality Provision in Bill C-20," a research paper prepared for the Federal Task Force on Broadcasting Policy, November 1985; Report of the Task Force on Broadcasting Policy (Caplan-Sauvageau) (Ottawa: Minister of Supply and Services, 1986), p. 147.

26. Bruce Owen, *Economics and Freedom of Expression: Media Structure and the First Amendment* (Cambridge, Mass.: Ballinger, 1975), pp. 107, 138-9. See also Bruce M. Owen, *The Internet Challenge to Television* (Cambridge, Mass.: Harvard University Press, 1999).

27. Caplan-Sauvageau Report, pp. 176-7.

28. Ellis, p. 59.

29. Quoted in C. Hoskins and S. McFadyen, "The Economic Factors Relating to Canadian Television Broadcasting Policy: A Non-technical Synthesis of the Research Literature," *Canadian Journal of Communication*, 12 (1986), p. 30.

30. Senate Committee on Mass Media (Davey Report), Vol. 1, *The Uncertain Mirror* (Ottawa: Minister of Supply and Services, 1970), p. 257.

31. Fraser, p. 136.

32. *Ibid.*, p. 135.

33. Quoted in McNulty, p. 191.

34. Fraser, p. 106.

35. *Ibid.*, pp. 277-80.

36. For a passionate critique of these decisions, see Herschel Hardin, *Closed Circuits: The Sellout of Canadian Television* (Vancouver: Douglas and McIntyre, 1985).

37. Caplan-Sauvageau Report, p. 40.

38. Keith Acheson and Christopher Maule, "Canada's Cultural Policies - You Can't Have it Both Ways," *Canadian Foreign Policy*, 4 (Winter 1997), p. 68.

39. Fraser, p. 254.

40. "Notes for an address by David Colville before the Standing Committee on Industry," February 22, 2000; CRTC website, www.crtc.gc.ca/ENG/NEWS/SPEECHES/2000/; accessed May 5, 2000.

Conclusion

1. Maurice Charland, "Technological Nationalism," *Canadian Journal of Political and Social Theory*, X (1986), pp. 196–220.

2. Morris Wolfe, *Jolts* (Toronto: James Lorimer, 1985), p. 111.

3. Report of the Committee on Broadcasting (Fowler Committee) (Ottawa: Queen's Printer, 1965), p. 3.

4. Ted Magder, "Going Global," *Canadian Forum* (August 1999), p. 15.

Index

MEMBER OF SCABRINI GROUP

Québec, Canada
2005